SAVING FIRE ISLAND
— FROM —
ROBERT MOSES
THE FIGHT FOR A NATIONAL SEASHORE

CHRISTOPHER VERGA

THE
History
PRESS

Published by The History Press
Charleston, SC
www.historypress.net

Front cover: Robert Moses (*at left*) and Babylon town supervisor Arthur Cromarty inspecting the construction of the Fire Island Inlet Bridge. *Town of Babylon Office of Historic Services Image Collection.*
Back cover, clockwise from top left: Bumper sticker that promoted making Fire Island a national seashore. *Karl Grossman Collection*; Four-wheel-driving on Fire Island beach. *Queens Borough Public Library, Archives,* Long Island Daily Press *Photograph Morgue Collection*; Aerial photograph of Fire Island in 1926. *Bay Shore Historical Society.*

First published 2019

Manufactured in the United States

ISBN 9781467140348

Library of Congress Control Number: 2018963594

CONTENTS

ACKNOWLEDGEMENTS

N o one person can own or monopolize the history they write or interpret. The gatekeeper to our history lies in the collective efforts of a community to keep it alive. Whomever we recognize as heroes or villains are defined as such by the impact they had on a community they represented. One person's hero can be another person's villain and vice versa. Robert Moses's undisputable impact was that he opened Long Island for suburban development, but Moses overlooked the environmental impacts on—and the destruction of—the region's traditional seaside communities. Diverse perspectives and resources are needed from various communities to tell this story.

This book would have not been possible without the support of Lillian, Susan and Catherine Barbash and Irving Like. Their interviews, pictures and documents helped me reconstruct the challenges and events that created a more environmentally conscious Long Island. The power of civics and citizen activism demonstrated by the Barbash and Like families created an organized, community-wide grassroots movement that is duplicated throughout the county. The Fire Island National Seashore, enjoyed by hundreds of thousands of people every year, will always be a testament to the legacy of the Barbash and Like families.

Special thanks to Lee Koppleman, who devoted hours of interviews to make this project successful. Kopplelman's legendary accomplishments are ingrained in his creations of Suffolk County Community College, Suffolk County's Environmental Bill of Rights, Blydenburgh Park and Gardner

Park. His lifetime work in attempting to create balance between economic development and conservation paved the way for grassroots activists to achieve success within the dawn of the environmental movement.

Special thanks to Mary Cascone and the Town of Babylon Office of Historic Services for sharing the images of Robert Moses, early barrier beach communities and construction of the Robert Moses Bridge. I would like to express my gratitude for the images of the construction of Jones Beach provided by Dr. Geri Solomon and Hofstra University Special Collections. These images are the backbone upon which the retelling of an almost forgotten history and heritage of Long Island is built.

I would like to extend special recognition to all the local historians I consulted with at the Fire Island Lighthouse Preservation Society, Bay Shore Historical Society, Babylon Village Historical Society, Nassau County Historical Services, Seatuck Environmental Association and Suffolk County Historical Society.

INTRODUCTION

T ranquil shorelines of sun-washed sands cover the turbulent history of man trying to dominate the elements of nature. The conflict of man versus nature is central to the argument of finding a balance between conservation and economic development. Through the limited resources bestowed upon inhabitants, conflict will batter ordinary people into ignominious obscurity—or turn them into legends. Unchecked political power and futuristic visions of a modern suburbia will collide with a bygone era struggling to hang on despite the changes created through fast automobiles and superhighways. Grassroots activism, pioneered in the 1960s to keep Fire Island environmentally and culturally intact, will become the catalyst for the modern-day environmental movement throughout Long Island and sink the career of the most revered man in New York State government, Robert Moses.

Fire Island's estimated thirty-two-mile length, and its width of over a half-mile at its widest point, keep nearly all resources in short supply. Despite its limits, the island provides unlimited tranquility for the 500,000 people who vacation on it each year. Able to endure the worst hurricanes ever to hit New York, the island was almost unable to withstand suburbia. With the 1962 Atlantic hurricane season fresh in the memories of mainlanders, coastal flooding became a central topic in the debate about planning for suburban development. The misconception that accessibility created by automobiles could democratize the natural beauty of South Shore's estuaries posed a threat to the rustic landscape and fragile balance of preservation. Fire Island as we know it today could have been a four-lane highway connecting Ocean Parkway to Montauk Highway in Montauk.

An estimated 450,000 cubic yards of sediment transported over 3,500 years of longshore drift steadily expanded into an isthmus that, by connecting current Fire Island to the Long Island town of Quogue, joined the islands into a peninsula.[1] Over a period of 200 years, longshore drift would grow the six-mile west end now known as Robert Moses Park and Democrat Point. Conflicting with the continuous growth are the 8,000 to 10,000 waves that strike the coast every day with an average rate of 313 to 417 per hour.[2] The effect of these waves is the erosion of the sediment from the shore and shifting shorelines. Diverse sediments created various vegetation habitats that include salt marsh, trees, shrubs and coastal plain vegetation such as beach grass. Over 300 years ago, Sunken Forest was created through the formation of two sets of dunes. This forest includes holly trees, cherry trees, black oak trees and sassafras.

An estimated ten thousand years ago, ancestors of present-day Native Americans migrated to and established a civilization across Long Island. In the seventeenth and eighteenth centuries, Dutch and English colonists classified the aboriginal residents of Long Island into thirteen tribes: the Canarsee, Rockaway, Merrick, Marsapeague, Secatogue, Unkechaug, Matinecock, Nesaquake, Setalcott, Corchaug, Shinnecock, Manhasset and the Montauks. These classified tribes shared a network of kinships and trade between most Southern New England Algonquin-speaking nations. These original Natives who had encountered Fire Island had already named the two sections of the island Seawanauke, translated to "land of shells," and Paumanauk, meaning "land of tribute." In settler William Tangier Smith's survey, exploration records and notes, eastern sections of Fire Island were described as marshlands connecting mainland Long Island to the barrier island. These marshlands allowed Natives access to Fire Island to harvest its marine resources. The most valuable of the resources the Natives harvested from the island was shellfish, not only for eating, but also for the shells, which were used as wampum—the main currency traded among the Northeastern Native tribes. Fire Island also provided access to the ocean's abundant hunting ground for whales. Natives would feed on the beached whales stranded on sandbars or hunt them off the coast. After the whale hunts, Natives would light fires signaling inland natives for more supplies or communicating the bounty they had harvested. In the shallower waters, Natives depended on menhaden, a fish used as fertilizer for the growing of vital crops.

Unkechaug Indians, who once harvested the shell beds of present-day Smith Point, standing outside of the Poospatuck Reservation. *Sandi Brewster Walker Collection.*

Production of wampum and menhaden made the local Long Island tribes' stable political structures wealthy through trade of resources harvested from Fire Island. The successful harvests of these abundant resources were due to the balance of conservation and consumption.

At the dawn of the seventeenth century, Europeans started colonizing Long Island. Interaction between the Native Long Islanders and European settlers grew to be problematic when it came to the definition of land ownership. The divide between Natives and Europeans came to a fatal climax in 1653. In western Suffolk and modern-day eastern Nassau County, tensions began to rise between the Marsapeague Natives, who lived there, and European settlers, who wanted to live there, creating rumors of potential raids against the European settlers. Under orders of the British colonial government, Captain John Underhill marched 120 men into a South Shore marshland called Fort Neck and slaughtered 150 Marsapeague men, women and children. From this time forward, Long Island Natives were passive to any of the European treaties or laws.[3]

In the early eighteenth century, Europeans began to take control of the island from the local tribes through a series of treaties. In 1658, Chief Wyandanch sold the eastern part of the barrier beach to Lion Gardiner. In March 1688, Chief Tobaccus sold the town of Brookhaven the rights to all whales that became stranded on the beach for five pounds of wampum.[4] Selling the rights to stranded whales decreased the value of the barrier beaches to many native tribes. European land ownership of the largest section of the barrier island was attained when William Tangier Smith purchased modern-day Smith's Point from the Unkechaug for 175 acres in mastic.

The growth of conquered land acreage created a demand for cheap labor, generating more difficulties for Native survival. Enslavement or indentured servitude of Natives reached its peak in the late eighteenth century. Throughout Queens County (combined Queens and modern-day Nassau Counties), 27 percent of residents owned an enslaved person. In Suffolk County, 18 percent of residents had ownership of a person. These numbers could be estimated on the lower end due to the number of slaves who could have been smuggled in through the ports to avoid taxes. Legend has it that Fire Island came to be used as a drop-off point for undocumented slaves who were later shipped to wealthy landowners across the South Shore. These sales of land and enslavement of Natives shifted the wealth accumulated from the island to the European settlers and the British Empire.

With the full change of ownership, the name of current-day Fire Island was based on localized sections of the island, such as Raccoon Island, Seal Beach or Siekrewhacky. The name Fire Island is believed to have come from a misreading of a Dutch map. The Dutch word *vier,* meaning four, was misread as *fier,* which was then further transmogrified into *fire.*[5]

The prominent issue the Europeans struggled with was the balance between harvesting resources to meet growing demands and conservation. Seals were abundant around the inlet, which led both local Natives and Europeans to name the area Seal Beach. The sealskins came with a high value for Dutch and English settlers. Within a decade of European control, seals became almost extinct. Following the overhunting of seals, whaling created an economic boom. Whalebone was used for brush handles and other fashion products; whale blubber was boiled, and the oil created fuel for lamp lighting during the Industrial Revolution. Within one hundred years of the commencement of commercial hunting, whales became a rarity, and many species came close to extinction.

One kind of vegetation that was grown on coastal barrier islands—and upon which European colonists became dependent—was salt hay. This natural hay grown on Fire Island was not only used for livestock feed but also as insulation for colonial housing. In 1784, the overgrazing of cattle and harvesting of beach grass and hay took a toll on the dunes. To stabilize eroding dunes, New York passed a law banning grazing, harvesting of hay and cutting of timber on Fire Island. Despite the ban, harvesting of salt hay and grazing continued due to lack of enforcement. Waterfowl across Fire Island and the surrounding estuaries became prized in the eighteenth to nineteenth centuries. Duck became luxury meat across the Northeast, and feathers from various fowl were used for pillows. By the dawn of the twentieth century, just as it had gone for the seals, almost all prized species of fowl had depleted populations.

As a result of the exhaustion of overharvested resources, Fire Island became a place of squatters and pirates. Increased shipwrecks and rumors of pirate activity that encouraged wrecks led to the construction of a 74-foot-tall lighthouse on the west end of the island in 1826. Employment of dependable lighthouse keepers became a challenge. The job entailed the person being isolated from mainland communities and enduring long, monotonous tasks. Early lighthouse keeper Felix Dominy became known for his innkeeper skills while serving as lighthouse keeper in 1843. A popular belief is that Dominy earned his innkeeper reputation because of the successful brothel he ran next to the lighthouse. Unable to slow the fatal wrecks owing to the small size of the lighthouse and the limitations of the lighthouse keepers, the U.S. Life-Saving Service built a station on the island in 1848. The Life-Saving Service station was manned by volunteers who patrolled the beach watching for distressed ships and smaller craft. Upon identifying a distressed vessel, the service then braved the elements and the ocean to rescue the crew and all others aboard the foundering craft. In the summer of 1850, a ship named the *Elizabeth* sank off the coast of Point O' Woods. This wreck became nationally known due to the death of women's rights activist Margaret Fuller. The attention attracted by this wreck brought national pressure to bear on the federal government to replace the 74-foot-tall lighthouse with a 168-foot-tall lighthouse in 1858.

The construction of the new lighthouse attracted real estate speculators and increased the number of disputes over land claims. Real estate magnate David Sammis aggressively started buying up the west end of the island and wanted to expand his ownership to the eastern part of the island, which was historically set aside as grazing land by various farmers. In 1871, a suit was brought against Sammis—*Green v. Sammis*—that challenged the legality of his ownership on the western and eastern tracts of land.[6] The ruling resulted in the Great Partition of 1878, allowing residential and commercial development and the opportunity for Sammis to build his luxury hotel—the Surf Hotel in Kismet.

Above: Fire Island Lighthouse keeper Richard Mahler's son going to school. *Library of Congress*.

Opposite, top: U.S. Life-Saving Service rescuing passengers of a distressed ship off the coast of Fire Island. *Bay Shore Historical Society*.

Opposite, bottom: Nuns clamming in the South Shore estuaries. *Library of Congress*.

☞ Persons engaging rooms will please state definitely the time they wil remain. Rooms will be charged for from the day they are engaged. Throug Tickets sold and Baggage checked to Hotel.

SURF HOTEL, FIRE ISLAND.

D. S. S. SAMMIS, Proprietor.

Advertisement for Fire Island's earliest resort, the Surf Hotel. *Bay Shore Historical Society*.

Fire Island's most sustaining commercial resources were the shellfish beds and schools of migratory fish. Large canning companies, followed by factory housing for workers, began to develop in the towns of Lonelyville, Fair Harbor and Seaview as a result of the 1878 court ruling. In the 1880s, Captain Selah Clock built the Fire Island Fishing Company in Lonelyville, Fair Harbor, and in 1895, the Gil Smith Fish and Canning Factory and worker housing were built in the community of Seaview. These factories were kept open thanks to the proceeds of the clamming and oyster industries. In the mid-1800s, the shellfish industry along the Great South Bay and Fire Island peaked at seventy thousand barrels per year and employed between three thousand and six thousand people on the South Shore. Similarly to what happened with the seals, whales and waterfowl, this resource was overharvested, but the hurricane of 1938 destroyed what little was left in the shell beds.

Rebuilding of the Fire Island economy depended on the scrabble to find a new resource. As the commercial fishing industry entered an economic

U.S. Life-Saving Service using breeches, a buoy and a series of ropes to rescue passengers of a stranded ship. *Bay Shore Historical Society.*

tailspin, tourism boomed. David Sammis's Surf Hotel proved to be a lucrative business, but in 1892, New York State was in the grip of a cholera scare and needed emergency quarantine stations. Consequently, during the fall of 1892, Sammis sold the Surf Hotel to the state for $210,000, with the state paying him $50,000 up front. With the success of the hotel and lack of competition (in many real estate and hotel financiers'

Above and opposite: Fishermen using gill nets to harvest fish in the bay. *Bay Shore Historical Society.*

minds), summer communities flourished across the island. This growth of the resort community resulted in seventeen communities that serviced different types of vacationers with cultural identity, artistic expressions, desires and fundamental religious needs. Communities of Point O' Woods, Cherry Grove, Saltaire, Ocean Beach and Dunewood would have the greatest impact on the future economic development and preservation of Fire Island.

During the 1890s, the chautauqua movement was spreading throughout the United States. This movement embraced adult self-improvement with conservative Protestant values. Point O' Woods, founded in 1894, based the development of its community upon exclusive access and chautauqua philosophies. Centered on the development was the policy of excluding Black people, Catholics and Jews. The town maintains isolation from other Fire Island villages thanks to the twenty-five-foot fence on the western part of the community. In addition to the fence, the town operates a private ferry service for community members, which furthers seclusion.

In the late 1960s, *Village Voice* columnist Nat Hentoff tested the exclusionary policies. Hentoff argued that the community of Point O' Woods is run like a private club, and the government should not be subsidizing private clubs. Hentoff attempted to gain access to the village post office but was denied. This denial resulted in a discrimination complaint that removed federally funded postal service from Point O' Woods. In an additional measure to limit any attempts to create diversity, the town property owners' association asserted that all residents operate on a 99-year lease. These restrictions were not imposed legally in accordance with the laws governing rentals and current land leases, but the limited access exclusions still affect the town's diversity by barring certain visitors. Over 120 years after its establishment, Point O' Woods remains the most insular community on Fire Island.

To the east of Point O' Woods, Cherry Grove was established in 1868 around the development of the Perkinson's luxury hotel. As early as 1882, the Cherry Grove community became a magnet for artists and bohemians. According to local lore, Oscar Wilde stayed at the Perkinson's Hotel and reportedly described it as "one of the most beautiful resorts" he visited.[7] During the 1920s, the renovated Perkinson's Hotel, now the Duffy Hotel, attracted city residents because of Cherry Grove's lack of a strong police presence and relaxed enforcement of Prohibition. This isolated island privacy also led to Cherry Grove becoming a resort town that welcomed homosexual guests—this development was attributed to the town's proximity to New York City's metropolitan center.[8] On mainland Long Island, resistance arose against the emerging community. The *Suffolk County News* and other local newspapers referred to Cherry Grove as "a moral danger," and the *Patchogue Advance* (published from 1885 to 1961) criticized locals who were not outraged over Cherry Grove.[9] By the late 1940s/early 1950s, the demographics of Cherry Grove property owners shifted to a point at which more than half of the homes were registered to gay owners. This demographic progression shaped the community into a well-known, openly homosexual resort community that provides its townspeople with a more democratic voice in local community restrictions and codes through the Cherry Grove Property Owners' Association. Through the collective efforts of the Cherry Grove Property Owners' Association, the seasonal residents successfully defeated a mainland Long Island antigay campaign. Famous visitors to Cherry Grove who helped bring the town's homosexual culture into the mainstream included Tennessee Williams and Truman Capote. The success of Cherry Grove shaped the 1947 development of

Aerial photograph of Fire Island in 1926. *Bay Shore Historical Society.*

Fire Island Pines. Known for its top-name actors and models, "The Pines" helped to develop the party reputation of Fire Island. Today, The Pines still embodies the party traditions of decades ago with the highest property values throughout the island.

Saltaire was originally formed in 1910, when Fire Island Beach Development Corporation purchased a one-square-mile tract of land from Henry Glahn. Advertised throughout upscale New York City real estate companies, Saltaire attracted some of the city's wealthiest people. The success of advertising increased the size of the development, leading to it becoming an incorporated village in 1917. During the early 1920s, a casino was built that specialized in serving alcoholic beverages during Prohibition. Similar to many locations across Fire Island, Saltaire was part of Hell's Kitchen gangster William "Big Bill" Dwyer's Rum Row territory. Like other towns across the island, Saltaire was used as a pickup location for a weekly average of 750 cases of liquor, which was shipped throughout the mainland of Long Island. The party reputation and picturesque beauty made owning a second home in Saltaire a status symbol. The reputation created a little over a century ago still holds firm today.

Ocean Beach was subdivided and marketed to city residents by John Wilbur in 1908. Increasing year-round populations created a demand for

The Creek   Bay Shore, Long Island, N. Y.

This page: Fire Island ferry terminal in Bay Shore. *Bay Shore Historical Society.*

a public school. In 1918, Ocean Beach opened the only school on Fire Island. Heirs of Judge Wilmot Smith merged the tracts of land known as Stay-a-While Beach and Ocean Beach in 1921 to incorporate the Village of Ocean Beach.[10] During the 1920s, the community's population makeup shifted from middle-class summer residents to artists, writers and young bohemians. The culture of the community became immortalized in the

Fire Island ferry the *Evelyn* traveling to Ocean Beach. *Bay Shore Historical Society.*

story and Broadway play *Season in the Sun*. Today, Ocean Beach is known for its variety of bars and nightlife that place it among top destinations for vacationers. To manage the hard-partying vacationers, the village created strict code enforcement. This strict enforcement led to it earning the nickname "The Land of No."

The community of Dunewood arose from marshlands and an illegal dumping site. Inspired by the natural beauty and rustic lifestyle, Maurice Barbash developed Dunewood into a family-friendly community with one hundred homes. For the price of $11,990 or more, anyone could purchase a three- or four-bedroom house. The community has no bars and a "no rental" clause to prevent parties that can conflict with family vacations.

The three communities east of Davis Park—Skunk Hollow, Whalehouse Point and Long Cove—were dissolved. These communities lacked electrical access and relied on hand pumps for water. Each community had an estimated fifteen houses or cottages. The oldest of the three was Whalehouse Point. Isaac Stratford, of Babylon, New York, founded the community that had been settled as far back as 1653. The community was utilized as a whaling station. All three communities were eventually leveled, and the property became a part of the Fire Island National Seashore's preserved wilderness.

The seventeen small communities that developed across Fire Island, with some consisting of as few as twenty acres, continue to remain isolated and fragmented in culture and identity. Differences in religious norms, political views and economic status restricted social interaction among residents to little or none. The only commonality was their love for the tranquil landscape and the need to take decisive action to preserve it by any means necessary. The collective efforts of strangers with very little in common—and their ability to unify—would determine the future of Fire Island's existence.

1

ROBERT MOSES AND HIS RISE TO POWER

Robert Moses planned and helped develop over 400 miles of parkways and bridges; 2,500,000 acres of developed parks; 658 playgrounds and over 150,000 housing units in the New York Metropolitan area. Moses's legacy is bound up in the cement used to construct his highways, parks and housing units people have used to live, commute and enjoy recreation in the late twentieth and early twenty-first centuries. Getting these many projects done required him to have almost unchecked power. When Moses lost his grip on power, he held twelve nonelected positions within state government. He kept himself safe from public opinion by influencing all major papers across the tristate area. The *New York Times* and *Newsday* kept stories flowing that were favorable toward Moses, arguing that his projects represented progress. With all his titles and freedom from accountability, Moses never received more than $25,000 in yearly income from New York State. His second–highest paid job was president of the World's Fair Corporation, which was contracted to him for five years with a total payout of $100,000.

His passion for power and his devotion to urban and suburban planning were matched by his love for the South Shore estuaries of the Great South Bay. As thousands and thousands had done before him, Moses fell in love with Fire Island and envisioned democratizing its natural beauty around accessibility to roads for weekend drivers.

The story of Robert Moses begins on December 18, 1888, in New Haven, Connecticut. His parents—Bella Cohen and Emanuel Moses—came from wealthy Jewish families. Bella came from a family of successful dry goods importers and real estate investors. Emanuel was a department store owner in New Haven. Robert's passion, drive and decisiveness were inherited from his mother, who performed a great deal of social activism work. After moving to New York in 1897, Bella became an enthusiastic funder and worker in the Henry House Street settlement but switched her focus to the Madison House.[11] At age sixteen, Robert finished secondary school and was admitted into Yale. There, he faced the reality that his religion would prevent him from breaking into Yale's major social clubs.[12] In 1918, Robert received his Ph.D. in political science from Columbia University and began to seek a career within local politics.

New York State secretary of state Robert Moses in 1926. *The Miriam and Ira D. Wallach Division of Art, Prints and Photographs, New York Public Library.*

Following the election of New York State governor Al Smith, Smith's top advisor— labor activist Belle Moskowitz—hired Moses to design reforms to make New York State's government run more efficiently. The proposed outcome was to consolidate 175 state agencies into 16 departments and to extend the governor's term from two to four years, with the aim of acting more quickly on state projects.[13] Smith lost reelection in 1920 but was elected in 1922 and kept Moses on as a staffer. During Smith's terms of 1922, 1924 and 1926, Moses created the Long Island State Park Commission and was appointed New York's secretary of state. Moses's first course of action in state government was to surround himself with loyal coworkers associated with his 1909 graduating class at Yale. Smith's tenure as governor did not last long. In the 1928 campaign, he was defeated by a member of his own party—Franklin Delano Roosevelt. Smith's defeat was due to his anti-prohibition views and a strong and growing bias against Roman Catholic candidates like himself. Roosevelt, maintaining many of Smith's appointees in their positions, kept Moses on, but Moses viewed the challenge from Smith's own party as a betrayal and held deep resentment against Roosevelt. For Roosevelt, the governor's position was a stepping-stone to the presidency, which he was first elected to in 1932. During the first years of his administration, Governor Roosevelt provided millions of dollars in funds for any public works projects that were shovel-ready. Implementation of Moses's proposed projects thrived. From the proposal stage to completion, every project Moses promoted was covered in the media and transmitted to the wider community. Every Christmas, Moses would enclose pictures of that year's completed projects in cards he sent to his friends and family.

Around Babylon Village, Moses became a well-known figure. Within the community, he would invite local veterans to go swimming in the salt estuaries, but as his success peaked, his presence would become more of a local legend. Moses became more ingrained in his work. Through his office on Randell's Island or the old Belmont Estate in North Babylon, Moses often worked sixteen-hour days. Business meetings outside the office were conducted at the Snapper Inn in Oakdale or La Grangia Inn in West Islip. Due to time constraints, Moses began taking his daily swims in Landon Thorne's indoor pool at his estate in Bay Shore. Converting to the Episcopal church, Moses began to attend St. Peter's by-the-Sea in Bay Shore. Parishioners within the church noticed that he started off like anyone else in the congregation but soon began to use the church as a means of building relationships with landowners and securing other professional transactions. Despite his passion for getting parkways, expressways and bridges built, Moses never got a driver's license and relied on a state-provided chauffeur.

Though the success of his projects continued, he became more aggressive about creating his highways, bridges and parks. Gradually, Moses became distant from his first wife, Mary Sims, as her health deteriorated in 1952. Moses's colleagues came to believe his obsession with his work provided him the opportunity to escape from taking care of Mary when she became bedridden. Following Mary's decline in health, Moses started to spend nights in his offices or his apartment in Gracie Terrace, Manhattan. While distancing himself from his wife, Moses became inseparable from his secretary Mary Grady.[14] After fourteen years of turbulent health problems, Mary Sims died, and within the same year, Moses married Mary Grady.

When he wasn't brokering deals regarding parks or highways, Moses devoted his time to surrounding himself with the team of subordinates he created through personal favors to classmates, allowing him to be autocratic in his decision-making. The reputation Moses manufactured for the media was that he was a man who gets things done by any means at hand. His reputation spread to various mainstream media outlets, giving Moses the ability to harness public opinion as a tool to promote his ambitions. Moses consolidated his power within the state government by requesting commissions instead of pay raises. His commissions were used to establish himself or the governor as the only people who could regulate his power.

Robert Moses presenting his urban renewal project. *Library of Congress.*

For the sake of urban renewal, he ordered the bulldozing of entire neighborhoods he deemed blighted. Moses constructed highways that were the most advanced for the time, although the construction led to thousands of displaced people having to scrabble for housing. He justified the displacement of these populations by referring to them as "animals" to his peers and dehumanizing their neighborhoods in the press.

When local politicians tried to block his projects, Moses used the media to collect loyalty and support from other elected officials to override any unfavorable decisions. With growing power, he became more sensitive to criticism of his personal life by responding more argumentatively and adopting a condescending attitude. When media outlets and preservationists would publicly criticize his projects, Moses would respond by saying, "Critics do not build anything." Moses would silence any dissent that stemmed from rogue reporting, which could have threatened his power or overall vision. An example of Moses's style of retribution was his retaliation against local reporter Karl Grossman. In 1964, Grossman wrote an article in the *Babylon Leader* comparing Moses's treatment of civil rights protesters at his World's Fair to Bull Connors, and in response, Moses got Grossman fired from his job and blacklisted by many mainstream papers.

2
MOSES'S VISION FOR THE BARRIER ISLANDS

During family summer vacations, Robert Moses and his first wife, Mary Sims, would stay and later take up residence at Thompson Avenue in Babylon. While establishing his residency, Moses became enchanted with the landscape of the Great South Bay and surrounding ocean beaches. Moses would engage in conversation with old bay men and sailors to hear their stories of unforgiving ocean currents, pirates and local Native American folklore.[15] A local legend that stood out to Moses the most was the story of pirate and mercenary Thomas Jones. In 1692, Jones acquired large tracts of land from the Massapequa Indians that would later become part of the southernmost part of Oyster Bay Township. After purchasing an old boat, Moses became attracted to a barrier beach he would later name Jones Beach. Moses would walk along the beach and not see another human on the white sand, which stretched unbroken for miles.[16] While walking these beaches, Moses would fantasize about walking in the same steps of Thomas Jones and ancient Native warriors on a hunt or gearing up for war. This local exploration and "salt life" culture influenced Moses's vision of a parkway traversing all the barrier beaches from Jones Beach, Gilgo Beach, Oak Island Beach, Captree Island and Fire Island to Montauk. This road would provide accessibility to the insular beauty and culture that lies to the east of the most densely populated city in America.

Moses's first accomplishment toward his vision for a scenic highway was the development of Jones Beach State Park. Originally named High Hill Beach, the 2,400 acres of land contained dozens of seasonal fishing shacks.

Many residents of High Hill Beach were able to trace their roots to the land as early as the nineteenth century. Original settlers were exporters of whale products. In the early twentieth century, locals shifted their exports from whale meat to harvesting migratory fish, eels and clams from the surrounding salt marsh for sale at fish markets in Freeport. During the summer months, locals made additional money ferrying New York City visitors seeking day trips from marinas in Seaford and Bellmore.

In 1926, Moses acquired the land for the state. Most of the homes were demolished, but ten homes were saved and moved to Gilgo Beach. The land encompassing High Hill Beach (later Jones Beach) came with a challenging engineering problem because it was only two- to two-and-a-half feet above sea level. When high tide rolled in, most of the 2,400

Aerial photograph of the estuaries surrounding High Hills Beach. *New York State Archives.*

Christopher Foster (*in the center*) was the engineer of the Jones Beach Causeway and State Park. *Hofstra University Library Special Collections.*

acres would be submerged. Moses's engineer, Sidney "Sid" Shapiro, used large dredgers to dig the boat channels, and with the excess forty million cubic yards of sand, he built the park twelve feet above sea level and filled in the vast acres of swamps. Park facilities were to be constructed with the balance of nature and nautical culture. Jones Beach bathhouses were built in the Italian Renaissance style, and the water tower was designed to replicate the style of the bell tower of St. Mark's Cathedral in Venice. A two-mile boardwalk along the beach was dotted with life preservers and ship cowl vents as wastebaskets along aluminum railings to give the feel of a boat deck. The central mall of the boardwalk was connected by a pedestrian underpass and had a mast of a ship with the United States and state flags greeting visitors. Embracing the commercialized images of Native American culture, Moses had an active Indian village built. In the village, Moses employed Rosebud Yellow Robe, of the Lakota Sioux tribe, to do reenactments or teach Native crafts. The original constructed parking lots had art deco ticket booths that assigned parking tickets to any of the twelve thousand parking spots.

Within its first operational year, the park received over 1.5 million visitors. The success of the park created a demand for more parkways to allow more accessibility to the scenic beauty of the barrier beaches. In an effort to appease a strong voting base, politicians allocated domestic and federal funds to the Long Island Parks Department for construction

This page: Construction of the Jones Beach Causeway Bridge. *Hofstra University Library Special Collections.*

of an extension to Ocean Parkway into eastern Nassau County and Meadowbrook State Parkway. Nostalgic memories of an era when visitors could walk along white sandy beaches without another human in sight for miles began to fade. Successful parks and highways were beneficial for the majority of nonlocal residents, but local people—who had lived, farmed, fished or vacationed on the land and sea for generations—slowly started to resent that outsiders dictated what should be the best use of their land.

Top: Original columns being constructed for the Jones Beach Causeway Bridge. *Hofstra University Library Special Collections*.

Bottom: Cement being poured for the Jones Beach Causeway. *Hofstra University Library Special Collections*.

Moses came into his first conflict involving the Ocean Parkway while proposing an extension into Suffolk County's barrier beaches. Suffolk County's population in 1900 was 77,582, and in 1920, it jumped to 110,246. The increasing population came into conflict over what was "necessary" development and what locals wanted to preserve. Similar to the county, Babylon saw a population increase from 7,112 in 1900 to 11,315 in 1920. In 1856, the rural town of Huntington, which is now Babylon Township, encouraged the development of resort communities

Aerial photograph of the Jones Beach traffic circle under construction. *New York State Archives.*

on the barrier islands of Cedar Island, Oak Island, Oak Beach, Captree Island, Gilgo and West Gilgo Beach. Local officials leased property at low rates in hopes of creating resort jobs. The largest resort on these tracts of leased land was on Muncie Island. Once privately owned by the Muncie family, the land was divided into a luxury hotel and, decades later, a tuberculosis sanitarium.

At the dawn of the 1920s, the resort communities began to face an economic downturn that created opportunities for the state to take ownership of private property through eminent domain. Acquiring Oak Beach would come as the biggest challenge owing to its dense population despite the economic downturn. Rumors of Moses's Ocean Parkway cascaded fear into the hearts of property owners and vacationers on the western Suffolk County barrier islands. Alleviating their concerns, Moses assured Babylon officials that the state was not interested in land at Oak Beach or Oak Island and that the land could only be transferred by vote.[17] After his public assurances to Babylon officials, Moses secretly went back on his word and argued that state

Aerial photograph of Jones Beach State Park's fields four and five. Both fields were designed to hold a maximum of twelve thousand cars. *New York State Archives.*

Jones Beach Causeway Bridge open for nautical traffic. *Library of Congress.*

Above: Eastbound and westbound sections of the Jones Beach Causeway Bridge. The bridge tower is art deco architecture with nautical carvings on Ohio sandstone. *Library of Congress.*

Jones Beach Causeway Bridge. *Library of Congress.*

Photograph of the Central Mall and the iconic water tower. The water tower is 150 feet tall and made of Barbizon brick to resemble St. Mark's Campanile in Venice. *New York Public Library.*

The east bathhouse was built in the art deco architecture style. *New York Public Library.*

ownership of the town barrier beaches was essential for storm protection and for the construction of an emergency evacuation route to connect the mainland. Under pressure from concerned voters, Babylon town officials hesitated to endorse Moses's plans for connecting a road through Oak Island and Oak Beach. Moses, frustrated over the lack of political and public support, contested the legality of the land ownership claims of Babylon on Oak Island and Oak Beach. His argument was that when Babylon seceded from Huntington Township in 1872, the proper paperwork was not filed for the barrier beaches, making them state-owned land by default. Babylon officials, realizing the validity of the state's claim, compromised with Moses. The parkway extension was added as a referendum item, and the town would retain ownership over the property. In response to Moses's strong-arm tactics, the local newspaper, the *Babylon Leader*, started an anti-parkway campaign and demanded the town block any sale of the island or beach to the state. James Cooper's editorial in the March 30, 1928 issue of the *Babylon Leader* urged voters:

> *Vote NO next Tuesday on the park and road. The* Leader *has pointed out that it would take residents of Babylon twice or three times as long to reach Oak Beach by high power auto as it does by slow motor boat, and we wish to remind you that the town forever loses control of the land. It will give away town rights to hunting, fowling, and fishing, which has been bestowed to us from a patent by Queen Anne and the town trustees.*

Refining his original argument for the referendum, James Cooper publicly argued at town meetings that the struggle was about big government overpowering the sovereignty of local landowners, and that support of the bill would "give away the town's priceless heritage to an imperial government in Albany." Influential resident and Gulden's Mustard owner Frank Gulden took out a full-page ad in the *Bay Shore Journal* calling the road "an invasion the voter can block by voting No." In response to Gulden's criticism, Moses wrote an editorial to local papers stating, "Gulden is associated with mustard bottles and hot dogs, and to this date there does not appear any reason why he should be consulted. I have suspicion that his ad was written by an inmate over at Central Islip Psychiatric."[18]

Similarly to the proposed project, the election was just as controversial. Babylon was in the center of a demographic change. New residents coming from urban settings to Babylon were state workers. Moses used his influence to get the votes for his highway and to sway the reelections of town officials

This page: Muncie Island became the site of a wellness sanitarium, which utilized recreation on the bay as therapy. *Town of Babylon Office of Historic Services Image Collection.*

Many parts of the barrier islands had squatters who made a living harvesting shellfish. *Town of Babylon Office of Historic Services Image Collection.*

who had gotten in the way of his plans. On Election Day, Moses had all local state workers take breaks throughout the day and arranged rides to the polls for them in state-owned vehicles to vote for his proposal and his chosen candidates. The unified voting bloc of state workers pushed for the passage of the proposal. The final tally of votes was 1,063 "for" to 988 "against." In a follow-up to the election, James Cooper stated in his daily editorial:

> *Tuesday a scant majority decided to deed away a good portion of Babylon's birthright. The decision to confiscate property should have been left up to people who are not only taxpayers but also who are transient and have absolutely no interest in the place. Many of these never saw the beach, which they surrendered. The verdict was nothing short of a crime and hope it will be declared illegal.*

With the media criticism, pressure was put on newly elected and incumbent officials to slow the land transactions and compromise with landowners. Sections of Oak Beach cottages were to be spared from destruction if homeowners agreed to reduce the size of the contracted leasehold property to a size of 100 by 100—or a little less than a full acre—lot, with a total of 344 lots. Residents of Oak Beach were pressured to accept the compromise from the state after being surprised at the speed at which the state closed the Oak Island Inlet with no warning. Closing the inlet was the first step to make way for the parkway and end the insular communities where so many enjoyed a tranquil quality of life. The Oak Beach and Oak Island section of the highway was completed in in 1934, and to recoup some of the state expenses, a fifty-cent toll was charged to nonresidents to enjoy the landscape of the once-popular resort community.

Following the opening of Ocean Parkway, Moses wasted no time before obtaining land for a central-to-eastern Suffolk County extension. The biggest obstacle he faced regarding the extension was underestimating the force with which the people of Fire Island would oppose him as compared to the people of Oak Beach. When Moses became the commissioner of Long Island State Parks, the only state-owned land designated a park was located on Fire Island. The Surf Hotel and the surrounding land were purchased by New York State in 1892 for use as an emergency cholera quarantine station. In 1908, the danger of a cholera epidemic passed, and the state made the station into a park. The land west of the lighthouse was federally owned. This land was deeded over to the state in 1924. East of this acquired land were seventeen towns and villages. The largest populations within these villages were in Ocean Beach (205 people) and Saltaire (64 residents). The other Fire Island hamlet populations were 72 within Islip Township's jurisdiction and 42 in the Brookhaven Township's jurisdiction. Compared to the relative ease with which Moses had displaced Oak Beach and Gilgo Beach's combined population of 175 residents, it would be more of a challenge to displace people on Fire Island.

Moses's original argument for the extension and possible displacement of Fire Island residents was that the road would be an elevated dune road that would hold the dunes in place. This elevated road would then provide inland homes with protection against hurricane flooding. Promoting the idea of flood protection earned him the endorsement of Long Island's biggest real estate companies and speculators. William Enequist, president of the Long Island Real Estate Board, publicly supported the parkway by taking out an advertisement in the *Brooklyn Daily Eagle* that encouraged real estate owners

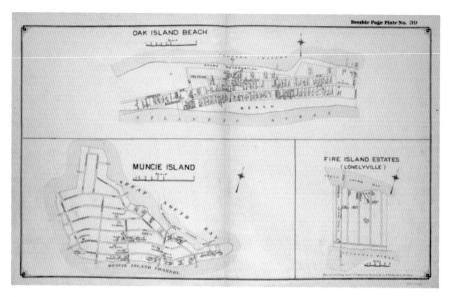

Community maps of Oak Island Beach, Muncie Island and Lonelyville (aka Fire Island Estates). These communities would have the proposed Ocean Parkway constructed through their village limits. *Hofstra University Library Special Collections.*

to sell their tracts of land to the state. While trying to gain as much local support as possible, Moses promoted the idea of highway commerce to the Long Island Chamber of Commerce, seeking its endorsement. In response, the Long Island Chamber of Commerce published editorials in the *Babylon Leader* stating, "the construction of the parkway and accessibility to the ocean front will raise property values across the South Shore." Real estate companies such as Gleeson and Dolan Development Corporation and the owners of Ocean Bay Park were influenced by the Long Island Chamber of Commerce and the Long Island Real Estate Board to willingly sell their land holdings to the Long Island State Park Commission. Not wanting to stand in the way of economic progress, Coulter Young, president of and major landholder in Point O' Woods, offered to his sell his personal holdings and advocated that the community's property owners do the same. Moses publicly blamed critics of the land sales for standing in the way of community growth for selfish reasons.

This wave of successful willingness to sell came to a standstill over disputes regarding land ownership. The most disputed land was an underwater tract. One tract of land adjacent to Heckescher State Park had ownership claims from up to three owners, including some of the richest people in the United

Sketch of Moses's Ocean Parkway, which would be built on top of the barrier island dunes. *Fire Island Lighthouse Preservation Society.*

States: Horace Havemeyer of Domino Sugar, W. Kingsland Macy of Macy's Department Stores and E.K Hutton of General Foods Corporation.

The delayed public push to sell land created enough time to form an equal amount of resistance. Media outlets such as the *New York Evening Post* published columns that stated things such as:

> *Fire Island's principal charm is that a few people know about them, and second that it is unprofitable for New York Telephone Company to run a line there. To escape from the telephone for a period of days, weeks or months is one of the rarest modern pleasures. The only menaces to the island's isolation are the Long Island Park Commission.*[19]

The villages of Saltaire and Ocean Beach hired legal counsel who waged a public relations campaign against the road. The campaign created a public relations movement that centered not only on preserving tracts of unspoiled land but also preserving a way of life that escaped the reality of urban sprawl. Counsel to the villages Leroy Iserman reaffirmed this image in the *Brooklyn Daily Eagle*, stating: "Fire Island is one of the few places within striking distance of New York where a man can go with his family and have unmolested peace and where his property rights are not tampered with." The success of preserving the island as a means of preserving a way of life started to make gains with property owners. The largest landowners who refused to sell were the Smith sisters of Point O' Woods. Reluctant sellers such as the Smith sisters and increasing legal challenges from land claims became the final blow to Moses's planned Ocean Parkway extension into Fire Island. Having no taste for defeat, Moses would become obsessed with

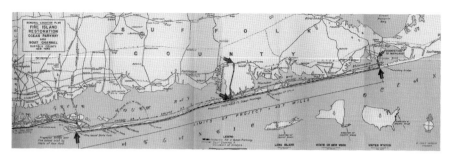

Map of Moses's proposed Ocean Parkway extension through Fire Island. *Fire Island Lighthouse Preservation Society.*

building his proposed parkway through Fire Island throughout the decades to come. While waiting for a shift in public opinion, Moses focused on other winnable battles during the war to construct his scenic parkway.

Moses's momentum for extensions of his Ocean Parkway project into Suffolk County was not limited by the short-term defeat at Fire Island. Parkway planning and construction increased when he was awarded $400 million in federal highway appropriations for all of his projects across the tristate area. Under the new federal appropriations, New York State proposed parkway and expressway projects that capped the cost to the state at $22 million. Moses set aside $4.5 million to connect the Southern and Northern State Parkways to Ocean Parkway by building a causeway through Islip resident David Gardiner's donated land. That highway became the Sagtikos Parkway and connected a causeway that linked to Ocean Parkway Captree. But state ownership of Captree Island came with challenges—not from private residents but from colonial town boundaries.

In 1931, Babylon deeded over 502 acres of land that comprised the largest tract of Captree Island. Captree had a small population of residents, but since 1899, Babylon locals wanted the area preserved for public recreational purposes; however, the state wanted the land preserved but with accessibility for automobiles. Despite the shared vision to preserve Captree, conflicts arose over a road's impact on preservation efforts as well as the town in which the parkway would be built. Babylon and Islip Townships provided land leases to residents on Captree Island, which complicated where Islip and Babylon Township property ended or began. During December 1930, Islip sold 81 acres of Captree to the state. In dispute were the hundreds of acres of underwater property on which the causeway would be constructed. The original William Nicoll patent of 1688 that created the Township of Islip stated, "all those islands, small sandy isles, marsh or meadow on the south shore between the inlet is William Nicolls (Islip Township land)." The patent was not clear on underwater ownership or rights. The full purchase of the land remained delayed until 1938, which came with an ownership compromise between the two towns. After Captree's ownership was transferred to the state, Moses turned his focus back toward Fire Island property owned by the state as a means of inching closer to an extension that would traverse the center of Fire Island.

The accessibility of the barrier island beaches created a demand for a boat channel and a stabilized inlet. East of the Fire Island Lighthouse, Democratic Point was part of a five-mile landmass that grew through seventy-five years of coastal longshore drift. The landmass continued to grow, shift and close any inlet or boat channel. The limited access to inlets and channels from the construction of the parkway fueled the $750,000 construction of a jetty. The completed five-thousand-foot jetty would be at the end of Fire Island State Park (currently Robert Moses State Park). Support for the construction was embedded in the goal of preventing further erosion of the Oak Beach community. The inlet expanded east and west instead of the original north and south direction. This east and west growth cut large landmasses from Oak Beach. The jetty would stop the coastal drift by keeping large amounts of sand from filling the inlet and boat channel.

In September 1938, Suffolk County waterfront residents endured a storm of immense waves and flooding that left a trail of carnage and destruction in its wake. The hardest-hit areas in New York were the Hamptons and Fire Island. Prior to the storm, developers across Saltaire and Cherry Grove had removed sand dunes to prevent any obstruction of an ocean view. This left these towns vulnerable to high ocean waves or storm surges. Fatalities from the storm were heightened due to the inability to prepare for the oncoming hurricane. The National Weather Bureau did not expect the hurricane to travel to New England in less than ten hours, nor did the Weather Bureau receive any sea reports of oncoming storms from vessels at sea.[20] The decision—based on aesthetics and not common sense—and the inability to prepare for the unusually fast-moving hurricane would bequeath a fear tangled into a tragic story.

As Fire Island residents prepared to end another great summer season, four hundred people remained on the island, including fishermen extending season gains or people winterizing houses. On September 21, 1938, at 2:20 p.m., a storm began to sweep over Fire Island. Most residents believed the coming storm was a nor'easter or a tropical storm from a weekend hurricane coming up from Jacksonville, Florida. Much to the surprise of the residents, however, the winds had reached 120 miles per hour, and waves had reached ten feet higher than normal in the ocean by 4:00 p.m. The overlooked storm developed into a Category 3 hurricane before slamming into Fire Island with full force. In less than an hour, the ocean waves reached thirty feet high before breaching the dunes of most of the towns on Fire Island.[21] As the storm reached its peak, ferryboats became stranded in the bay from the high waves and other navigational hazards. Newspapers across the nation reported Captain Gustave Pagel's heroic evacuation of residents before the storm reached its peak. His ferry had thirty-nine passengers departing from Fair Harbor when the waves made the bay impassable. An hour-and-a-half ferry ride became an all-night cruise of uncertainty for the crew until passengers were safely docked the next day at 9:30 a.m. In Saltaire, an entire section of ninety houses was washed out to sea, and another fifteen houses were damaged beyond repair. Four residents were killed: Mrs. Hass, Mrs. Bassine and her sister Alice, who were dragged away by waves washing over their home, and a woman identified as Francine who was reported to have been blown out the window. Ocean Beach and Seaview—a little over a mile away— did not have any casualties, and only four homes were washed away. The difference between these two communities was that Saltaire had leveled its dunes, while Ocean Beach and Seaview had kept them intact. Cherry Grove—another town that had leveled its dunes—had eighty-five houses wash away but no causalities.

The aftermath of the hurricane impacted the geographical layout and population of the island. Geographically, the storm cut ten new inlets along the South Shore. Populations in all the island towns plummeted. In 1930, Saltaire had 64 residents, but after the storm, it had 22. Saltaire's population remained in the low 20s until 1960. Prior to the storm, the Village of Ocean Beach had a population of 205, but it dropped to 81 after the storm and further declined—to 73 people—in 1950. The fatal outcome and population drop gave Moses a new foundation for his parkway argument.

Following the devastation caused by the hurricane, Moses used the people's fears and anxieties to further his proposal for his Fire Island Parkway. Pro-Moses editorials appeared in the *Babylon Leader* stating that "fewer people would want to utilize the land on the waterfront for building and should gladly lease the ocean front land to protect further water development."[22] Local papers entangled stories of the fatal hurricane into endorsements of any Moses project as a way to promote the highway and downplay its

This page: The effects of the 1938 hurricane on Saltaire, a village on Fire Island. *Bay Shore Historical Society.*

A house washed out to sea by the 1938 hurricane. *Bay Shore Historical Society.*

controversy. Moses quickly developed a beach restoration proposal for which federal public works grants and state bonds of $15.5 million were to be spent. Moses proposed hydraulic fill along the oceanfront that would be secured by dredging a boat channel on the bay side of the island, planting of beach grass to reduce dune erosion and a forty-three-mile parkway from Fire Island Inlet to South Hampton. Additional construction in the plan would create four state parks and four toll bridges. To promote his plan to the county, Moses led the Islip and Brookhaven town supervisors on a tour along Saltaire, to inspect the devastation, and then to his project—Jones Beach. Unlike Saltaire, Jones Beach had maintained its dunes, which protected the town from all but minimal damage, but Moses contended that it was the parkway that had kept the embankment of dunes in place. The *Babylon Leader,* which had the most critical editorials of Moses's Ocean Parkway, wrote on September 28, 1938:

> *Many do not favor the Oak Beach connection to Ocean Parkway; nevertheless, it is generally conceded that the height to which the road was built would limit the rushing water from the ocean into the narrow tip of the island, which might have sand fill it. However, had the road*

not been built, the tip of the land would have been much wider, and the rush of water might have been held back by the sand through the brush and the meadow.

The *Babylon Leader's* other argument—that the highway had no deterrent effect on flooding storm water—received little attention from other local papers but might have influenced the majority within Babylon Town Council. Moses made a final attempt to push his proposal, writing to his loyal supporters about how the argument should be framed. In an October 29, 1938 letter to Warren Greenhalgh, Moses said:

The Silly temporary, makeshift brush and fence work now being done with relief and other forces, where the dunes were wiped out along the ocean, will not survive the Ides of March! People are living in a fool's paradise, misled by millionaires with protection of bulkheads and steel pilings, who have not helped their less substantial neighbors.

Outside of Babylon Town Council, supervisors Warren Greenhalgh of Islip, Edgar Sharp of Brookhaven and John Brennan of Smithtown publicly announced their support for the project and aggressively lobbied the seven other town supervisors for their support. A recorded meeting within the town described the events of the meeting:

During the vote by the supervisors to pass the Moses restoration proposal, Edgar Sharp pled with the board, "People of Brookhaven are fearful of what might happen on the mainland if immediate steps are not taken to stem the high tides. The tide is reaching unprecedented levels at Mastic and East Moriches." Town of Babylon supervisor Frederic Wood countered Edgar Sharp by stating, "His town board has instructed him to vote for protecting beaches, but to oppose any plan for building bridges connecting Fire Island to the mainland or a parkway along the beach." Wood then voted against the proposal.[23]

The town supervisor of Southold, Wentworth Horton, cited concerns over the additional $5.75 million that would have to be raised and stated that "it will not be on the backs of taxpayers in my town." The alternative plan proposed by Suffolk County highway superintendent Hermon Bishop called for the rebuilding of dunes using fencing and planting of beach grass. The total cost of his beach restoration plan was $1 million. The outcome of the vote was three supervisors voting for and seven against the Moses proposal. The Bishop plan was voted in and implemented.

In response, editorials were written in the *Brooklyn Daily Eagle* to pressure lawmakers to reconsider. Harold Willmott of Huntington wrote in a letter to the paper: "Although the cost of the salvation of Fire Island—the first and last line of defense of the South Shore—as proposed by Moses may seem high, it seems to me that it may prove ridiculously low if the penny-wise pound-foolish policy of Suffolk County elected officials continues."[24] Despite the pro-parkway campaign, rebuilding did not include Moses's parkway. The new inlets were filled, dunes were rebuilt and dune grass and shrubs were planted to strengthen existing dunes.

The coming of the 1940s would bring the onset of America's involvement in World War II. The wartime rationing of resources would delay the construction of Moses's projects. Moses's ambition for an Ocean Parkway extension through Fire Island did not fade but became dormant until the peak of the post–World War II housing boom. Postwar Long Island would face a population explosion followed by a development boom in infrastructure that would make Robert Moses and his projects household names throughout New York.

3

MOSES'S FIGHT AGAINST A
FIRE ISLAND NATIONAL PARK

I n the early 1950s, the development of suburbia was in full swing. Federal
money was flowing into any project that would connect the growing
populations and consumer market to the emerging automobile-based
culture. Transportation centered on the automobile was always Moses's
key component to his vision of a futuristic city. This vision for a new
city would unclutter the urban settings into a more open suburban plan
based on a system of roads instead of a transit rail system or pedestrian
walkways. Old buildings and shacks would be leveled with very little regard
to historical significance. The trend in highway-dependent cities and
suburbia was aligned with the doubling of motor vehicle registrations from
1940 to 1955.[25] The increase in automobile registrations was enhanced
by popular culture's romance with the automobile and its elevation to a
status symbol. Television and commercial media of the 1950s exalted the
automobile, calling it "The Spirit of America's Freedom," making nothing
out of reach and promoting middle-class accessibility. Moses's parks, such
as Jones Beach, Heckscher State Park, Captree State Park, Fire Island State
Park (later renamed Robert Moses State Park) and Sunken Meadow Park
were designed with automobile accommodation in mind, democratizing
the landscapes and progressing in lockstep with the aggressive emerging
culture.[26] Governmental demands for these designs and an improved
highway system exceeded Moses's ambitions, forcing him to revisit his
proposed projects that had been postponed, such as the Ocean Parkway
extension through Fire Island. Moses believed the postwar housing boom

and cultural shifts to automobile-centered developments would sway local public opinion in favor of his Ocean Parkway extension.

Following the postwar cultural shift, Fire Island endured some of the worst hurricanes on record in 1954 and 1955. As he had used the hurricane of 1938 to his advantage, Moses used the fear and devastation of locals to make his argument for a parkway. The only obstacles Moses prepared himself to face were the price increases of hydraulic fill and waterfront land. Moses's original proposals had a price cost of six cents per yard for hydraulic fill, but as demand for suburban developments increased, the price peaked at thirty cents per yard. Other rising costs of the projected parkway included the soaring property values. In 1938, Moses had priced shoreline property along Shinnecock Inlet and was quoted five dollars per foot. In 1954, the price of that same property had increased to one hundred dollars per foot. The increase in prices created another lengthy delay in acquiring the land at peak value. Real estate speculators, seeing opportunity in the inflated values, bought large tracts of coastal land and held off on selling them until they could get the highest possible return. Rewriting federal and state grants to reflect the rising and projected prices would be time-consuming. While reworking the costs, Moses used funds he had on hand and state-owned land to complete smaller and cheaper projects related to the completion of Ocean Parkway. One such project was the Captree Bridge. While completing the Captree Bridge project, Moses received very little pushback, and he took this as a message that popular opinion was on his side, so finances would be the only obstacles. Understanding that the new Long Islanders of 1950s wanted a lifestyle based on automobile accessibility, Moses envisioned a slowly evolving movement that combined the cultural nostalgia of a land trapped in time with a strong demand to reduce the environmental impact of suburbia on estuaries as the last gasp of air from a bygone era.

Keenly aware that the public opinion of the new 1950s-era Long Islander would be the key component in building a scenic highway, Moses became concerned about Fire Island's new zoning for commercial and residential developments. The more people who owned homes on Fire Island, the more people who would be displaced. Ceasing all new development would pose an obstacle to keeping his plans discreet, but doing so would make it easier to acquire the land. In a letter to the Town of Islip Board, Moses stated: "New York has a huge investment in Fire Island and the town should prevent an intrusion of shacks crowded on small lots, which is a result of lowering zoning standards." Moses was

Construction of the Robert Moses Causeway Bridge connecting West Islip to Captree Island, 1950. *Town of Babylon Office of Historic Services Image Collection.*

successful in convincing the Town of Islip Board to not lower zoning standards, but he brought upon himself public suspicion that he was going to renew his Ocean Parkway extension, which became known as the Fire Island Highway project. Congressmen Stuyvesant Wainwright strongly opposed the Fire Island Highway and began to mount an offensive via a public relations war to kill the plan for good. Originally from South Hampton, Wainwright was a relic from the old aristocracy. A well-known socialite in the Hamptons, he rarely socialized outside of his blueblood WASP circle of friends. Sportfishing and large country estates of the old aristocracy were centered on the bounty of resources from the ocean and bay. Growing development along the South Shore and Fire Island started to heighten the concerns of his peers that their inclusive way of life might become urbanized.

Above and opposite: Construction of the first trestle of the Robert Moses Causeway Bridge. *Town of Babylon Office of Historic Services Image Collection.*

In response, Moses reassured the public that he was not building a highway through Fire Island, but he continued to influence policy that would make future construction of a highway all the easier. But Moses underestimated his foes, thinking that the center of his new fight was on rich preservationists who vacationed on Fire Island, but he found ranged against him those in the dying profession of the South Shore bay man. This conflict heated up when fisherman and clammers began to unify over concerns that the Moriches Inlet was to be filled in. Years of erosion had been gradually filling the inlet, and within three years of neglect, the inlet had become virtually closed, and tides could neither bring fresh seawater into the bay nor take water from the bay to the ocean. The effect was

that over one million dollars' worth of shellfish died from eastern Long Island duck farm pollutants that had drained into a stagnant part of the bay.[27] Prior to the closing of the inlet, the flow of ocean currents into the bay flushed out pollutants, which reduced fatal impact to shellfish beds or spawning fish.

Charles Duryea, a Suffolk County legislator, along with Congressman Wainwright's predecessor, Ernest Greenwood, not only wanted the Moriches Inlet restored but also wanted a new inlet to be cut west of the Fire Island Lighthouse to clean out the bay. Moses, wanting the least number of inlets—and possibly even having the Moriches Inlet filled in to benefit a future highway project to traverse the middle of all South Shore barrier beaches—blocked state and federal funds intended to maintain and restore Moriches. In 1952, local officials agreed on a less aggressive proposal of constructing a groyne in an effort to stabilize the Moriches Inlet, postponing any new proposed inlet and dredging for a boat channel. The total cost of the project would come to $1,706,213, and as a compromise, the Town of Brookhaven would cover 25 percent of the cost.

To gather further support of bay men and rally waterfront residents in opposition to Moses by supporting the stabilization plan, Wainwright promoted the idea that keeping the inlet closed would be the first step for Moses in building a highway through Fire Island. In an effort to cement the federal funding needed for the proposal, Wainwright pitched the cost of the project to the House Appropriations Committee. Following the meeting, a majority of the members expressed that they would not fund an inlet for the benefit of "millionaires' yachts and sailboats."[28] Not taking the rejection lightly, Wainwright rebutted that the inlet would have an important civil defense function because the boat channels provide a civilian evacuation route. Building on the setback in federal funding, Wainwright continued campaigning to residents by urging that a Fire Island highway plan that closes inlets would be a "natural disaster that will make our once lively bay into stagnant death." Consolidating the concerns of the fishermen and residents, retired Coast Guard captain Eugene Osborn formed the Moriches Inlet Stabilization Committee. Captain Osborn and his committee generated community letter-writing campaigns that quoted Wainwright's "stagnant death" warning. In fact, Wainwright's dire "stagnant death" foretokening evolved into a clear guiding idea and catchphrase—Save the Great South Bay. This was easy to remember, and it created a sense of urgency to join and back the cause. Concerns of residents spilled over to town hall meetings, and phone lines were jammed up within the town, county and state offices. Residents' demands to reopen the inlet mounted. The public pressure did not sway Moses, but it encouraged county officials to start emergency dredging operations to stabilize the inlet. In protest, Moses declared that Wainwright's plan "would be equivalent to pouring millions down a rat hole every year for maintenance."[29] Despite Moses's opposition, local and state officials started dredging in an effort to fully restore the inlet.

In an effort to build on the momentum of the grassroots anti-highway/ inlet-stabilization activism, Congressman Wainwright announced plans to introduce the proposal for a national park on Fire Island. Support for the national park won the backing of Secretary of the Interior Fred Seaton, who

WESTERN UNION

JUNE 28, 1957

HON. W. AVERELL HARRIMAN
EXECUTIVE CHAMBER
ALBANY, NEW YORK

STRONGLY URGE YOU NOT TO PRESS MORICHES INLET ADDED ITEM

IN HOUSE BILL. PLANS NOT READY. FINANCING ENTIRELY BY

FEDERAL PEOPLE UNUSUAL AND OPPOSED BY BUDGET, ENGINEERS

AND OTHERS. WILL INVITE OTHER ADDITIONS AND RESULT IN VETO

OF ENTIRE BILL. MOREOVER NO TIME IS SAVED BY INVITING

COLLAPSE OF FIRE ISLAND INLET AND ALL THE REST OF THE

PROGRAM.

ROBERT MOSES

CC: Mr. Spargo
Mr. Howland
Mr. Shapiro

Library

Telegram from Moses to New York governor Averell Harriman asking not to press any funding to maintain the Moriches Inlet. *New York Public Library, Robert Moses papers.*

openly endorsed the plan. Seaton was eager to welcome the plan due to a National Park Service report that cited that only 6 percent of seashore from Maine to Texas was publicly owned. This report motivated the Department of the Interior and federal officials to set a goal of 15 percent public ownership. Moses immediately went on the defensive.

Moses started a letter campaign to Conrad Wirth, director of the National Park Service. In an August 16, 1955 letter to Wirth, Moses stated:

> *Acquisition of any land east of the state park is hopeless, not only because of local opposition but because of the increase from 6 cents a yard for hydraulic fill to 30 cents a yard. There is no possibility of constructing a highway at a safe elevation. Thirty-seven miles of the South Shore coast are protected. Finally, let me say that the real problem is on the North Shore, where there are no state parks on fifty miles of the shore from Sunken Meadow and Wildwood State Parks.*

In response to Moses's letter, Wirth wrote, "we have no plans at this time on acquiring any of Fire Island for a National Park, but seashore reports about shore line protection have created concern." This response infuriated Moses. Moses called on local and state officials to write to Wirth and tell him that preservation is on track along the South Shore and his focus should be on the North Shore. In editorials, Moses explained the opposition to federal interest of a national seashore was an argument over whether New York was capable of preserving the oceanfront. Using the federal support, Wainwright held town hall meetings with his constituents to sell the idea. Many of his constituents' attitudes differed on the national park idea. Residents strongly supported the preservation of Fire Island but expressed concern over large New York City crowds intruding on the day-to-day life of locals or possible conflicts in regulation for commercial and sports fishermen. Within the Fire Island communities, a lack of communication with homeowners about the benefits of a national park had filled the void with speculation. Moses, using the disapproval of the national park to kill Wainwright's proposal, asked New York governor Averell Harriman to make a public stand against the national park. Moses's reason for the governor to be opposed to the national park was that "unlike the Federal Government, New York has 30 percent of the waterfront in public ownership and turning the property over to the federal government will limit any demand for future development."[30] Governor Harriman's response to Moses was vague and stated that he would not give a public endorsement for or against the park. On the defensive, Moses went over the governor's head and wrote to New York senator Jacob Javits. Moses reminded Javits of all the land he put in public ownership and told him not to support the federal park, the proposal of which was becoming a bill. Doubling down on reintroducing his highway to Javits, Moses argued

Aerial photograph of the season's peak tourist traffic at Jones Beach State Park. *New York Public Library.*

that the "strip of land that makes up Fire Island is narrow and receptive to damages and needs an elevated dune road to protect Long Island from storms and erosion."[31]

While forming a coalition against the national park, Moses began seeking public ownership of property on Fire Island from people who had large land holdings. Walter Shirley owned Smith's Point—eight miles of the eastern end of Fire Island (now Smith's Point County Park). On June 23, 1959, Shirley agreed to donate large tracts of the land to any future parkway project. Sections of Shirley's eight-mile stretch of donated land had construction underway for a marina and zoned parts of the bayfront for residential housing. For property owners like Shirley, a highway would allow access to any future bayfront luxury homes. Building this alliance between the developer and the master planner became even stronger with Suffolk County executive Lee Dennison's desire to extend the county tax rolls.

Moses's use of the lack of communication that fueled suspicion among Fire Island residents inflamed fierce public campaigns against the federal park regarding the idea of property rights. The prospect of federal ownership of Fire Island came with an easily marketed fear and distrust stemming from the concept of an overbearing federal government restricting landowners' property to the National Park Service. Outside of the Eastern South Shore communities and Fire Island, the national park idea received less media traction and public support. Wainwright's argument for seashore preservation was for the protection of a secluded way of life instead of a focus on natural areas. This argument and resistance from Moses made the national park idea an uphill battle. Successful preservation of Fire Island and an indefinite ban on Moses's highway would have to start within all the Fire Island communities and be exported to the mainland. The success of the imported message on preservation would have to be based on its benefit to the entire community—not a select few.

The argument highlighting seclusion and not preservation was damaging to the Wainwright reelection campaign. The first congressional district had some of the largest population growth in the country at the time. Conflict between new residents and old residents was growing due to the shift in demographics. Seizing on the opportunity to get rid of a political adversary, Moses rolled out his classic argument of elitism against Wainwright's preservation proposals. On November 8, 1960, Wainwright was defeated by Democrat Otis Pike.

The failed reelection campaign of Wainwright and national park proposal might have fallen short in terms of support, but it had moderate success in building a solution to future conservation challenges. A preservation movement that developed on Fire Island would be exported to the township, county, state and federal levels. The cornerstone of the environmental preservation movement would not be a battle for seclusion but a battle of science waged by Dr. Robert Cushman Murphy—an ornithologist with the American Museum of Natural History. Murphy, who summered in Point O' Woods, introduced the concept of creating a "living museum" as the reason for preserving the land. This living museum required the least amount of impact from man and would challenge Moses's idea of preservation through increasing accessibility for the automobile. After Murphy's publication of *Augusts on Fire Island,* the indispensable natural value of Fire Island became a front-and-center issue among New York naturalists. With the growing interest in the fading waterfront habitat, Murphy started a chapter of the Nature Conservancy on Long Island. The first call to action from the Nature Conservancy was the preservation of a tract of land east of Point O' Woods named Sunken Forest. Murphy and the Nature Conservancy organized Point O' Woods property owners and garden clubs across lower New York to collectively purchase Sunken Forest in a trust.[32]

Funds to maintain and expand the property were raised with the help of Murphy's wife, Grace. With her networking ability, she created an alliance with Conservationists United for Long Island and the League of Women Voters to access local foundations and endowments. In an outcome similar to what happened with the community of Point O' Woods, the success of preserving Sunken Forest came with limited access to the public.

The Moses argument against elitism would be his greatest asset to beating back preservationists. Moses's success in constructing his argument would depend on the fragmented cultural divides that isolate people from one another. Murphy's grassroots efforts, successes and failures inspired a scientific preservation movement, but it would still have to evolve and unify against any argument waged by Moses in order to be successful.

4

DEVELOPMENT WITH LIMITATIONS

After World War II, Long Island witnessed its largest economic boom, which was fueled by construction of the largest suburban developments in the country. This building boom occurred for three main reasons. The first and dominant factor of the boom was the Servicemen's Readjustment Act (the G.I. Bill), which provided guaranteed low-interest mortgages for sixteen million World War II veterans. Benefits to demilitarized soldiers and a reforming of Federal Housing Administration (FHA) guidelines that had made homeownership attainable created a housing shortage of five million homes throughout the country. The second factor was the failure of Long Island's staple crops, such as the potato. Potato fields across Long Island came under attack from an insect called the golden nematode as well as falling prices from crop surpluses. The third factor was the developed highway system throughout Long Island. Robert Moses's parkways had begun to open up the interior of the island to traffic, enticing builders to buy land.[33]

The best known large-scale development, Levittown, was constructed on the Hempstead Plains of Nassau County. The flat surface and low brush of Hempstead Plains were ideal for the construction of more than seventeen thousand Cape Cod homes. The homes marketed an image of a suburban garden in the country. Streets were named after bushes, trees and flowers, and well-manicured lawns and hedges lined the widening blocks. Along the South Shore, Cape Cods similar to those of Levittown remained the houses of choice for developers due to the flat land. As demand grew for homes that were in balance with the scenic landscape, developers turned their focus to the North and South Shore coasts. Construction design of housing had to adapt to challenging terrain. The popular 1950s split-level home was designed for steep and sloping land, which was common along the North Shore.[34] In the mid-1950s, tracts of buildable property increased in value. Marshlands remained cheap to developers, and many included views of the waterways. This combination led developers to adjust to the varied configuration of the land for housing construction. Thousands of acres that made up marshlands and estuaries were drained or paved over for developments to fulfill the ever-increasing demand for houses with views of the water.

The residential housing boom was not the only economic development changing the landscape of Long Island. Prior to World War II, Long Island had begun to attract an aviation manufacturing industry to meet the needs of the military airbases established along the Hempstead Plains. The outbreak of World War II had tripled aviation-manufacturing output. To keep up with demand, defense companies expanded manufacturing and engineering jobs, which generated a demand for land. Grumman, Republic, Fairchild and Sperry opened factories from Lake Success to Calverton. By 1945, over 100,000 Long Islanders worked in the defense manufacturing industry. After World War II, the Cold War was at full throttle, maintaining the demand for jobs and land. Construction of projects such as the Lunar Module, F-14 Tomcat and the Thunder Jet led to the need for a highly skilled and salaried workforce, catapulting thousands into the middle class with disposable incomes. With all the focus on job growth and technological advancements, proper commercial waste disposal and protection of groundwater and waterways were not considered priorities.

The housing developments and air defense industry across Long Island attracted the largest population increase in New York State history. In Nassau County, the population in 1940 was 406,748, but within twenty years, it had jumped to 1,300,171. In 1940, Suffolk County had a population of 197,355, but less than twenty years later, the population had swelled to 666,784. Within another ten years, Suffolk County's population would nearly double to 1,127,030. This growth made Long Island's gross domestic product (GDP) larger than the GDP of nine southern and midwestern states combined.

With all the new state parks being created in an effort to keep up with demand, the suburban lifestyle that attracted millions of new residents started to include more urban congestion and pollution. Manhattan's congressmen John Lindsay once joked, "I do not trust air I cannot see," referring to the smog in New York City, but in the 1960s, urban populations brought the same pollution problems of the city with them to Long Island through increasing automobile exhaust, illegal dumping of waste into waterways and overdevelopment of housing. Families migrated to Long Island for a lifestyle that provided a balance with nature and had an abundant amount of open space for kids to play. In less than a decade, thousands of families faced destruction of nearby open spaces, robbing their children of beloved places to play.[35] By 1970, more than half of all land in Nassau and Suffolk Counties had been developed for residential use. As an agricultural hub for lower New York, Suffolk County had over 123,000 acres of farmland in 1940. Within less than twenty years, the county's total farmland dropped to 80,000 acres. A little less than 25 percent of the county landmass used as farms was rapidly becoming rededicated to housing and strip malls.

The rapid development not only destroyed natural forests and open space but also caused environmental disasters. For years, Moses had filled in marshlands as a means of mosquito control and to utilize open land for parking lots or parkways that cut through his parks. Overlooked was the ecological purpose of the wetlands. Tidal wetlands work as a filter

Aerial photograph of the completed Jones Beach Causeway. *New York State Archives.*

removing toxic sediments from the estuaries and offer breeding grounds for fish and protection from erosion and inland flooding. The greatest loss to wetlands was in the Long Island Sound area, which endangered North Shore communities, as it exposed them to toxic runoff and flooding. By 1970, 31 percent of the Long Island Sound's and 48 percent of New York's total wetlands were lost due to overdevelopment.[36] In addition to the loss of wetlands, the Long Island Sound was suffering from unregulated dumping of waste products. All along the North Shore, "more than 1 billion gallons of sewage was dumped into the Long Island Sound every day from New York City, Long Island, and Connecticut public works."[37] Building along bluffs on the Long Island Sound eroded storm barriers and protection from coastal flooding. The once elaborate North Shore communities started to view their waterfront neighborhoods as liabilities instead of hubs of rest and recreation.

Along the South Shore, residents attracted by its legendary prize game fishing found fish populations decimated through overfishing and toxic storm water runoff. When it rained, the Long Island Sound and Great South Bay absorbed city industrial waste products such as *benzene*. Septic tanks and cesspools—installed by the hundreds in new housing developments—started to overflow and harm beloved creeks and town beaches. Intestinal bacteria plagued beaches, causing skin and ear infections for swimmers. High levels of coliform (bacteria found in fecal matter) became so common that by 1960, original safety regulations that had been set at 240 in each 100 milliliters of water was increased to 2,400 in each 100 milliliters of water.[38] Southeastern Nassau County's Biltmore Beach reached the highest levels of coliform bacteria in the state, averaging 4,580 for each 100 milliliters of water. Babylon's Sontapogue Creek and Frederick Canal became visibly polluted and plagued the surrounding areas with a pungent odor. The creeks were inspected, and the culprit was runoff of household chemicals and runoff from cesspools. When political officials were questioned about the increasing amounts of pollution generating health concerns, they collectively responded, "The contamination seems to be coming largely from runoff that is nearly impossible to stop."[39] Moses himself started to take notice of the pollution when he was told to stop taking his morning swim in a creek behind his Thompson Avenue house because of a possible risk of getting a gastrointestinal virus.

The greatest environmental scare came in the late 1950s with the contamination of groundwater from manufacturing. Nassau County residents struggled with a constant lowering of the water table resulting from a growing population, but now the question arose as to whether the water was safe to consume. Commercially used detergents were found in the table as deep as seventy-two or more feet, and it would be impossible to filter out for safe use.[40] Eastern Long Island drinking water wells started to be at risk from dichlorodiphenylchloroethane (DDT) contamination. DDT—a pesticide linked to various forms of cancer and fetal abnormalities—was used for decades in factory farming. However, once a well has been contaminated, DDT's harmful effects may persist for more than fifteen years.[41]

At the dawn of the 1960s, elected officials, once shielded from polluted parts of the county, began to take notice of the formerly abundant resources becoming scarce within their own communities. Wild turkeys became extinct due to lack of open grazing space; the once wide variety of hawks and ospreys started to disappear because of the toxic DDT pesticide, which caused defects in their eggs; and the piping plover disappeared from the beaches due to development of the oceanfront. These now visible effects could not be rationalized as a part of progress, and public opinion made public officials react. Calls for environmental action from grassroots activists and homeowners' associations were intensified by Rachel Carson's book *Silent Spring*, which drew public attention to the effects of growing development encroaching on nature's treasures and the potential environmental disasters that would follow.

Silent Spring, together with growing public concern about the visible environmental changes, shifted not just public opinion but also the culture of suburban Americans' responsibility. Legislation was created for responsible land use and to obtain public ownership. Prior to 1960, Suffolk County would have large tracts of land go into tax default, and local towns rushed to subdivide the land and sell it to developers who would put it back on a tax roll. After the collective awareness, larger tracts of land in Suffolk County started to be examined by officials for ecological importance before rezoning.

At first, Suffolk County planners viewed the population growth as a blessing, but they became concerned when projected population growth for the county could potentially reach 3.3 million by the mid-1980s. This explosion in population could have more dire effects on quality of life through exhaustion of natural resources. Taxpayers and homeowners' associations across Long Island demanded the preservation of land surrounding their communities and organized town hall events that invited politicians to address their concerns. In Suffolk County, legislators passed an Environmental Bill of Rights, which created a commission to review all planning within the county to determine its environmental impact. The new environmental commission gave top priority to the protection of remaining unspoiled estuaries. These local protections did not just limit building in marshlands but banned it.

In 1960, the environmental concerns were not confined to just Suffolk and Nassau Counties. New Yorkers voted overwhelmingly to approve a park bond for $75 million.[42] Following the success of an open-space bond, a state bond for $1 billion was added in an effort to create a sewer district that would end sewage polluting rivers, lakes and salt estuaries. Governor Nelson Rockefeller argued that "nearly two-thirds of the state's population lives in polluted areas, with sewage as the main pollutant."[43] The billion-dollar, ten-year program would finance the construction of sewage treatment facilities.

Long Island's increasing environmental concerns and activism were exported to a federal level when Suffolk County residents formed the Environmental Defense Fund. The new organization established a platform of seeking a national ban on DDT and working to preserve vital ecological habitats. The Environmental Defense Fund evolved to become an aggressive lobbying group that not only put environmental issues front and center in local elections but also brought them into federal political debates through endorsements of laws and political candidates. Smaller, localized bird-watching and other nature clubs consistently organized letter-writing campaigns, endorsed candidates with pro-environmental agendas and expanded their influence by seeking support of influential people across the country. Lawrence Rockefeller, one of the wealthiest and most politically well-connected people in the United States, became an ally to the Environmental Defense Fund's local groups and bankrolled many of their political campaigns.

Consolidating activism to gain influence at the national level launched a shift in policy to redesign growing suburbia and recreation spaces. New York State officials scrambled to intermix the environmental concerns of Long Islanders with growing suburbia, but Moses—always betting against the odds—was still fighting for a design that he had envisioned in the late 1920s.

5

THE DEFEAT OF MOSES
AND THE MAKING OF A NATIONAL SEASHORE

L ong Island society was rapidly changing. Collective concerns for the environment and questioning of governmental authority became the center of evolving state policy. In the past, whenever Moses had faced opposition to his vision of the automobile-dependent park, he crafted his argument as a "Fight against Elitism"—the mechanism that barred the common person's access to the natural landscape. Moses perceived his designs of parks that allowed greater accessibility to the automobile as a symbol of twentieth century Americanism. In reality, his vision promoted un-American access by limiting his parks to only middle-class people who were able to afford automobiles. Car-based culture became not only a tool to reinforce economic and race-based segregation but also a force destructive to natural habitats and historic communities. During the mid- to late 1950s, the preservation and automobile-centered paradox would be brought into public debate, and demands to redesign suburbia would gain traction.

Moses's projects within New York City were killing traditional urban life. Activists successfully rallied and preserved Washington Square Park and other historical landmarks within Greenwich Village. Across Fire Island's villages and towns, a growing population of residents of New York City's Greenwich Village took up summer residences, bringing their activism east to the barrier island. Local residents waged oppositional arguments against Moses, such as whether preservation of parks through pavement could have irreversible effects on an already strained ecosystem. Moses's Jones Beach project had preserved the oceanfront and the beaches

Jones Beach Causeway Bridge base under construction. *Hofstra University Library Special Collections.*

but destroyed—for parking lots or parkways—any maritime forests or salt marshes that might have existed in the area. Locals began to notice that parks like Jones Beach clashed with the wilder nature of Long Island before it was populated.[44] Unlike Moses and his projects, conservationists and activists were evolving with a message that could reach the average person facing environmental and quality of life changes. Moses's response to the growing environmentalism and activism was, "These ecologists are Johnny-come-lately. At Jones Beach if we waited for the environmentalists, the whole goddamn place would be covered in small cottages by now."[45] Moses's arrogance and his not accepting the growing concerns of environmentalists became his greatest challenge to any futuristic city impregnated by parkways that cut through scenic landscapes.

The late 1940s and early 1950s brought a new type of vacationer to Fire Island. Similar to bohemian artist colonies of the 1930s, in the 1950s, Fire Island attracted writers, painters and a new demographic of environmentally conscious, upper-middle-class people gradually embedding themselves into the Fire Island community. Vacationers were no longer attracted only to scenic landscapes but to the opportunity to mingle with well-known artists, writers or actors. Similarly to Long Island itself, the act of having visited or honeymooned on Fire Island became an ingrained status symbol. Thousands would record memorable moments to be displayed in photo albums in homes across the United States, putting this formerly secluded island in the mainstream. Advertisement through shared pictures was followed up with nostalgic stories of romantic walks on the beach during majestic sunsets while sharing drinks with world-renowned celebrities, expanding Fire Island tourism to new heights.

Maurice Barbash, originally from the Bronx, had a strong desire to live a life that balanced outdoor leisure with living space. As a child, Barbash had ridden the subway to Brooklyn to explore the surrounding wetlands of Coney Island. While observing the natural habitat of the wetlands, he became interested in bird-watching and joined local nature clubs. With a strong desire to live a suburban life, Barbash had met someone else whose drive matched his—Lillian Like.

A few years after Maurice and Lillian were married in 1947, they went on a date to see the Broadway play *Season in the Sun*. The island backdrop, where people had no automobiles and limited access to communication, allowing them to fall off the grid, intrigued them. This backdrop was almost a fantasy compared to the 1950s reality of fast automobiles, expanding cities and growing addiction to accessibility for the purpose of communication.

This almost unimaginable place—Fire Island—became the center of Maurice and Lillian Barbash's getaways. While exploring destinations to visit on the island, they noticed ads in some village and town newspapers that featured churches within the community. Jewish couples like the Barbashes understood that ads like these were a dog whistle meaning "No Jews Allowed." A popular community that had no such ad was Ocean Beach. When the Barbashes first visited Ocean Beach, they were starstruck at discovering all the literary figures and famous actors within the community. Movie stars like Marilyn Monroe were known to walk up and down the strip along the bay to watch the sunset. Mel Brooks and Carl Reiner would walk along the ocean to find their inspiration. Staying at Housers Hotel by the Bay, the newlyweds were invited by well-known writers to join them for drinks. Accepting the invitations, they witnessed discussions and debates among some of New York's most notable intellectuals in smoke-filled rooms over scotch and other whiskeys. During these get-togethers, noted war correspondent Theodore White would randomly drop by to discuss contemporary political issues.

Based on Barbash's observations, the friendly, welcoming and intellectual culture of Ocean Beach was not confined to its borders. Maurice found equally surprising the different identities that developed after World War II in the surrounding communities. Ocean Beach—a more outgoing and friendly community—was the opposite of the inward-looking, old-wealth community of Point O' Woods or the exclusive nouveau riche community

Left: Ocean Beach vacationer leaving the ferry terminal. *Queens Borough Public Library, Archives,* Long Island Daily Press *Photograph Morgue Collection.*

Below: Fire Island town of Fair Harbor on the bayside. *Queens Borough Public Library, Archives,* Long Island Daily Press *Photograph Morgue Collection.*

of Saltaire. The community of Kismet was open to anyone, but it was a working-class culture of hard-drinking local day-trippers. Many Kismet residents viewed the community of Ocean Beach as pretentious city people and had very little interaction with Ocean Beach or other surrounding communities. In turn, these local biases toward city people or artists kept many non–Long Islanders away from the community. The communities of Fair Harbor and Lonelyville attracted a more integrated community of established artists and successful city businessmen trying to keep low profiles. The eastern Fire Island town of Cherry Grove was a growing gay community that became stigmatized as a place for what local media called "an island of undesirables." This growing antigay sentiment reached its peak in the 1950s with the high-profile murder of a wealthy man. The murder became a catalyst for the Rockville Center Catholic Diocese to encourage Catholic churches to contact their local police to discourage the growing gay population. Throughout the 1950s, local police led raids in Cherry Grove, arresting same sex couples for "lewd acts." Fear of the raids kept the Cherry Grove community isolated from the surrounding towns. Cherry Grove's community activism combated this antigay sentiment by focusing on property rights for gay homeowners. East of Cherry Grove, Fire Island Pines and Davis Park had a flood of artists flocking to rustic homes with limited utilities in an effort to escape the hustle and bustle of New York City. The Davis Park and Pines crowd were some of the legendary patrons of the 1950s White Horse Tavern. Within these Fire Island towns, borders were enforced through economic status and the culture of materialism that set invisible boundaries. To most middle-class people from outside Long Island or New York City seeking refuge on sun-soaked beaches, these towns were little more than resorts with no identity, but once they became acquainted with each community's culture, the boundaries became visible.

Following the Barbashes' visit to Ocean Beach, Maurice asked his brother-in-law Irving Like to come with him to explore Fire Island and its astonishing landscapes and individualistic communities. While walking the shores, Maurice and Irving found a stretch of land between Lonelyville and Fair Harbor that was being used as a local dump. However, Barbash envisioned a family community that would become a sanctuary from the hard partying of Ocean Beach. This community would not allow rentals, would have a tennis court, would offer separate ferry service and would feature homes designed around the landscape. The layout would have one hundred homes clustered to maximize community green space. The maximizing of green space would be presented as a marketing balance

The main strip of Cherry Grove, Fire Island. *Queens Borough Public Library, Archives,* Long Island Daily Press *Photograph Morgue Collection.*

between preserving Fire Island's landscape and feeding economic demand for private island paradises under the sun and by the water. The homes would come in two models—the Sandpiper and the Dolphin. The Sandpiper would have three bedrooms, and the Dolphin would have four, and each would come with a wraparound deck. No bars or sales of alcoholic beverages would be permitted in the community. Historic prejudices and racial covenants kept Fire Island a secret from many Jewish families, but now it would have a community available for anyone with $11,990. The sales brochure for every home stated, in bold capitalized letters: "ALL RELIGIOUS SERVICES ARE OBSERVED." This development—like Moses's initial goal of opening Fire Island's great landscapes to the common man—would democratize Fire Island home ownership.

Throughout the rediscovery of Fire Island in the 1950s and early 1960s, vacationers grew concerned about maintaining and preserving the island. Communities outside of Point O' Woods formed activist groups with the goal of maintaining the island ways of life. Leaders of these groups had to balance the collective potential of seventeen communities on the island. These leaders represented some of New York's most powerful business owners; best public relations executives, writers, editors, actors and artists; wealthiest families and most feared lawyers.

The valuable network of visitors was not confined to the island. On the island and the mainland, elected officials began to notice the generated tax revenue from the homes, which utilized close to no public works. Economic benefits of this exclusive reputation kept rentals booked and ferries packed with vacationers who brought more political influence along with their affluence and large amounts of disposable income.

The surrounding South Shore communities of Bay Shore and Sayville had their downtowns prosper thanks to people passing through to the ferries. Boatyards, which were slow during the year, made their entire revenue for the year during the peak Fire Island season from Memorial Day to Labor Day. The Bay Shore and Sayville Chamber of Commerce found a way to collectively form a successful consolidation of power among businesses that prospered from the seasonal visitors. The chamber of commerce soon generated a strong political influence on local and state elections. Building an organization that consolidated various concerned citizens, their influence and their wealth, the Bay Shore and Sayville Chamber of Commerce established influential power locally and was able to extend its sway to the federal level.

Left: Maurice Barbash and his daughters Cathy and Susan standing in front of the "Welcome to Dunewood" sign on Fire Island. *Susan Barbash Collection*.

Below: Aerial photograph of Dunewood. *Susan Barbash Collection*.

The Sandpiper model, which includes three bedrooms, was one of the types of homes built in Dunewood. *Susan Barbash Collection.*

The Dolphin model, which includes four bedrooms, was another type of home built in Dunewood. *Susan Barbash Collection.*

The first challenge would be to unify the seventeen communities with a set of shared guiding ideas. Following the hurricane seasons of 1954 and 1955, resident Gil Serber established the Fire Island Erosion Control Committee. Maintaining the well-known sandy beaches of the island served the interest of all its communities and businesses. This group successfully advocated for erosion-control projects and funds from the federal government to reduce flood damage on private property.[46] The success of the erosion control projects allowed the group to target broader preservation efforts to maintain the tranquility of the island. An example of the group's effort to guard serenity was its resistance to the Town of Islip's attempt to build a paved access road through Fire Island towns within Islip's jurisdiction. Many residents of the island viewed this planned road like one of Moses's parkway proposals. In response to these feelings, residents broke down the invisible barriers of income, social class and sexuality to become a unified front. The result was that one thousand residents and vacationers came to a public hearing in Ocean Beach to block construction of the access road. The swiftly organized resistance and attention from the residents killed the proposed paved access road and showed the mainland elected officials that the island could unify. In an effort to keep the activist momentum fervent, Gil Serber and Arthur Silsdorf formed the Fire Island Voters Association (FIVA). The defeat caught the attention of Moses. He used the backlash of the proposed road as a measurement of public opinion. This helped him decide to keep the proposed highway a secret until another storm or hurricane could shift public opinion. Despite the efforts to keep up the momentum of activism, leaders struggled with residents falling back into their insular communities and resuming the maintenance of their social barriers.

To prevent a resurrection of the proposals for a national seashore for Fire Island, Moses turned his focus toward making Congressmen Otis Pike's ideas conform to his (Moses's) vision of an automobile-centered Long Island. Developing Pike as an advocate for federal support could boost funding for and implementation of Moses's projects. The representative from New York's First District was traditionally Republican, but a change in demographics created a population that was newer to Long Island and moved to the region because of its automobile accessibility. Moses believed this shift in demographics, along with residents' dependency on the automobile, would form the core support for Congressman Pike. In a manner similar to the Babylon town election that gave Moses the land for his Ocean Parkway, Moses used loyalty from his state workers to sway the election, but now Moses had popular support and the loyalty of a congressman. After Wainwright's defeat, Pike took a stern position against any possibility of a national seashore. This gave Moses the opportunity to push through his proposal for the Fire Island Inlet Bridge. Moses wrote up the estimate for total construction costs as $9.8 million. In a letter to Robert MacCrate, counsel to the governor, Moses stated, "Under Federal Aid Highway Act of 1958 the 90 percent Federal share payable on road projects will be increased by ½ percent if the state enters in an agreement with the Secretary of Commerce before July 1, 1961. If we fail to get this passed New York will lose millions of Federal Aid dollars."[47]

Following his successful lobbying of state officials, Moses turned his attention to local media outlets. Moses wrote editorials in local papers stating he had no plans to make a parkway through Fire Island, just a bridge to the state park beaches. To convince skeptical reporters, he would invite them to dine with him at local popular restaurants such as Snapper Inn or La Grange to express their concerns. During his dinner parties, whenever he faced criticism about his original plans for Ocean Parkway, he would become aggressively defensive and change the topic to his current plans. Rumors of his Fire Island Parkway circulated among the elite in Point O' Woods. Notable lawyer Waldo Hutchins Jr. wrote to Moses, stating, "It would be a calamity to build in the unspoiled Sunken Forest. The state should provide protection to Fire Island estuaries or follow Cape Cod and become a National Seashore."[48] Moses replied to Hutchins, stating that "a National Seashore will not be necessary because Sunken Forest is a local park. At present over a third of New York's Oceanfront is publicly owned, which is an excellent record."[49]

The planning of the parkway on Fire Island remained secret. All memos to other planners related to the Fire Island parkway were marked confidential. Moses would take helicopter trips over Fire Island to identify large vacant tracts of land. Then, having identified the land he wanted, Moses would work with Suffolk County executive Lee Dennison to have the county purchase as many of these tracts as possible without attracting public attention. On November 21, 1960, the secret planning of the proposed parkway was almost leaked in a conversation between Dennison and wealthy landowner Robert Gardiner. In a memo to Moses, advisor Sid Shapiro stated, "Dennison has been talking about a continuous road on Fire Island. Is Dennison playing all sides? He won't enjoy a long public life if he is that kind of fellow. A premature Fire Island story would be damn near fatal."[50] Moses guarded as secret all planning of the parkway in response to a growing environmental movement across Fire Island and the

Construction of the Fire Island Inlet Bridge. *Town of Babylon Office of Historic Services Image Collection.*

mainland. The right timing to sway mainland support was being weighed against a bad hurricane season.

The opportunity to sway support for the Fire Island road came with the devastating headlines of March 6, 1962. Fire Island was hit by a nor'easter known as the Ash Wednesday Storm. The storm destroyed forty houses across Fire Island and sixty houses across the South Shore Coast of Long Island. Public opinion began to show concern about repeated flooding of the South Shore estuaries and waterfront towns. In a response similar to those he shared after previous hurricanes and storms, Moses reached out to all media outlets to sell to the public the need for his road. In a March 26, 1962 *New York Times* article, Moses explained that "his road would be similar to a dike to resolve the age-old problem of flooding."[51] With pressure from the public, the state formed the Commission on Protection and Preservation of the Atlantic Shore Front.

The objective of the commission was to come up with a comprehensive plan for combatting the recurring storms and hurricane damage. Seizing on an opportunity, Moses volunteered to cochair the commission with Ocean Parkway extension supporter Lee Dennison. The conclusion of the commission's study had five main points:

- *In order to protect this area even as a wildlife reservation it would be necessary to pump in a huge hydraulic fill for dune restoration of an 18-foot elevation.*
- *It would be impossible to maintain any policy without a road.*
- *Large portions of beachfront available for taxation would have to be removed from county and tax rolls to transfer it to public ownership.*
- *The cost of a road from Fire Island State Park to Smith Point and replenished 18-foot dune will be $21 million. Half of the parkway cost will be picked up through Federal Highway Aid.*
- *Preservation of land on a federal level is unnecessary because the state acquiring Fire Island will be well over 30 percent of oceanfront in public ownership.*[52]

Above and opposite: Robert Moses (*at left*) and Babylon town supervisor Arthur Cromarty inspecting the construction of the Fire Island Inlet Bridge. *Town of Babylon Office of Historic Services Image Collection.*

To achieve the recommendations of the commission, full cooperation would be needed at all levels of government—federal, state, county, town and village.[53] The commission outlined the plan for governmental cooperation. The implementation of the plan would not only reduce shoreline flooding but also increase property values across all South Shore communities.

The commission did not originally include the rising value of property, which reached $200 to $300 per foot by 1962, owing to the increased price of dredging boat channels and the price of moving displaced homes. The amended cost of the project increased to an estimated $50 to $80 million. Once the budget for the plan had been modified, Moses added changes to the project in an attempt to appease island residents. The new plan added exit ramps leading to most of the seventeen towns across Fire Island. No additional parking spaces were planned for these communities to prevent a loss of privacy. The only areas designated for visitors would be Fire Island

LONG ISLAND STATE PARK COMMISSION
STATE OFFICE BUILDING
ROOM 2401
270 BROADWAY
NEW YORK 7, N. Y.

November 21, 1960

MEMORANDUM TO SIDNEY SHAPIRO

FROM ROBERT MOSES

Apparently Lee Dennison has been talking to the County and other planning people about a continuous road on Fire Island and about other phases of his grandiose park and parkway program. Bob Gardiner told me this. Is Dennison playing all sides? He won't enjoy a long official life if he is that kind of fellow. A premature Fire Island story would be damn near fatal.

/s/ Robert Moses

President

RM:DM

File
Library
Miss Tappan

Memo to Sidney Shapiro from Robert Moses demanding the need to keep the Fire Island highway proposal a secret and outlining what repercussions Suffolk County executive Lee Dennison can face for leaking the proposal. *New York Public Library, Robert Moses papers.*

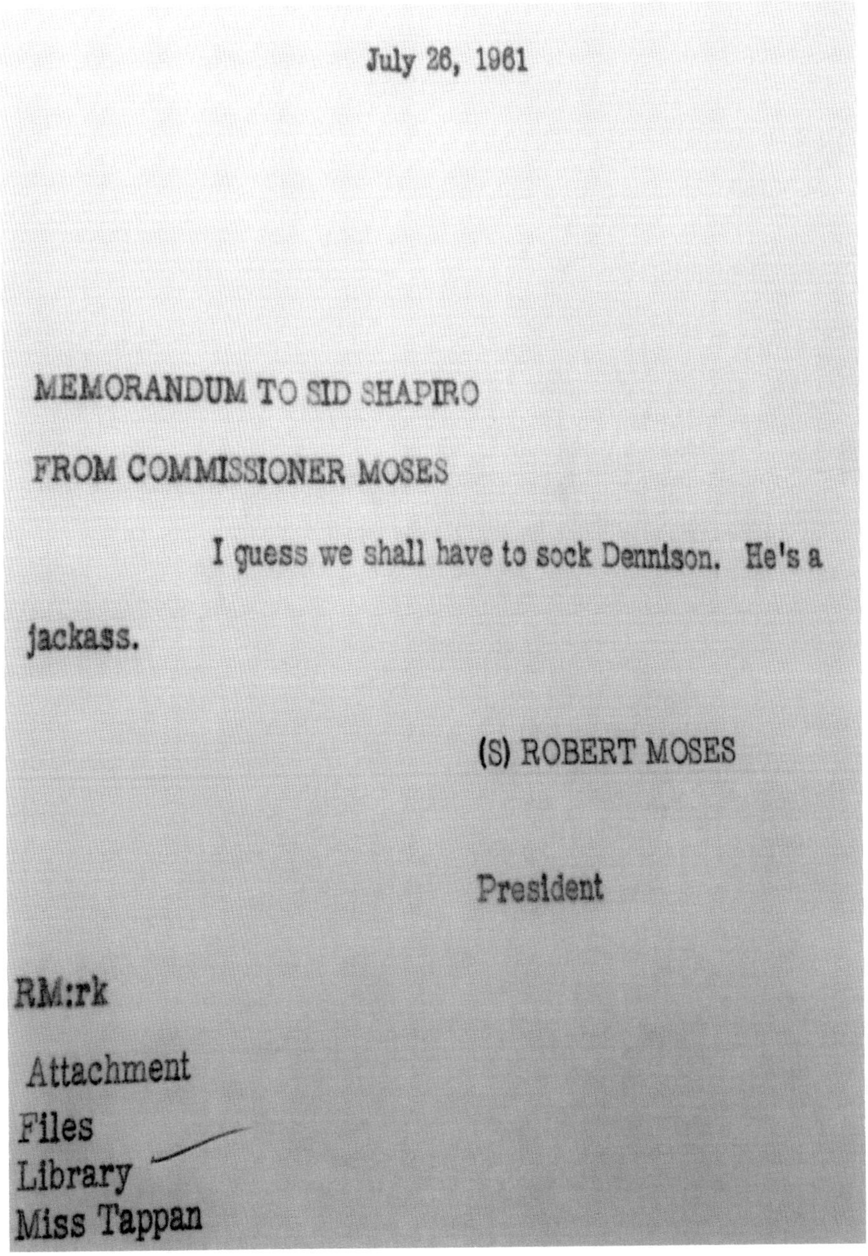

July 26, 1961

MEMORANDUM TO SID SHAPIRO

FROM COMMISSIONER MOSES

I guess we shall have to sock Dennison. He's a jackass.

(S) ROBERT MOSES

President

RM:rk

Attachment
Files
Library
Miss Tappan

Memo to Sidney Shapiro from Robert Moses expressing frustration over Lee Dennison leaking the proposal to the public. *New York Public Library, Robert Moses papers.*

Aftermath of the 1962 Ash Wednesday nor'easter. *Susan Barbash Collection.*

State Park and Smith Point. In an effort to reduce public reaction to the published report, Moses pushed the public hearing to July 10 instead of June 11. During this time, he was going to attempt to keep coverage of the plan out of the media. These attempts failed due to his most vocal opponent—Secretary of the Interior Stewart Udall.

Udall, who was familiar with Robert Cushman Murphy's work, shared Murphy's view of the need to preserve the East Coast barrier islands. Like Murphy, Udall believed that the preservation of national parks and the barrier islands should focus on maintaining the natural landscape over convenience and easy accessibility. Appointed in 1961 at the dawn of the environmental movement, Udall had his department review all vulnerable natural habitats. A 1955 federal study of the Atlantic and Gulf Coasts identified Fire Island as one of the most important remaining undeveloped shorelines in the northeastern United States.[54] Influenced by the report, Udall became determined to make Fire Island a federally preserved national seashore. However, Moses, recognizing the skepticism toward his plan at the federal level, invited Udall for a helicopter ride to survey the damage from the Ash Wednesday storm. At the conclusion of the meeting, Moses and Lee Dennison proposed to Udall that local, state and federal officials work together to preserve a tract of land east of Davis Park on Fire Island. Having neither committed to nor disapproved of the plan, Udall somehow left Moses with the impression that the federal government was in agreement. Udall's criticism of Moses's plans did not end with the helicopter ride. Strong support for his criticism was shared by the Fire Island Voters Association. In a letter to Arthur Silsdorf, the president of FIVA, Udall reminded the association of the options of the pending Shoreline Protection Act in providing $25 million in matching federal funds to buy land and that any achievement in conservation has to be agreed on at a New York and Suffolk County governmental level. In response to this letter, Silsdorf—now not only president of FIVA but also mayor of Ocean Beach—encouraged part-time residents to switch their permanent residence to Fire Island in an effort to give their communities a stronger political say on state funds and proposals for any road.[55] Silsdorf stated in an interview with the *Suffolk County News*:

> We pay taxes and we put large sums of our own money into erosion control and other services which municipalities ordinarily provide in return for taxes....But we have not had the votes....We will have a significant number of votes from Fire Island cast in the Islip Township elections this year.[56]

The letter from Udall to Silsdorf was leaked to *The New York Times*. Moses sent a telegram to Udall that stated:

> The letter between you and Fire Island Civic groups if true is a disappointment. These actions will create confusion and limit constructive action, which comes before an advertised public hearing. The federal government will be unable to accomplish anything without full cooperation of state and local officials.[57]

The lack of federal support was not compensated for at the state and local level. Local editorials throughout Long Island argued that a handful of people should not jeopardize the safety of a whole county from storms and flooding. Local incumbent support was almost unified, but political challengers took opposing stances. Congressman Otis Pike became a vocal supporter of Moses and his plans, but Walter Ormsby, Pike's Republican challenger, used support from local environmentalists to highlight Pike's lack of local environmental policy. Ormsby actively campaigned on the need to create a national seashore on most if not all of Fire Island. Ormsby argued that building a road through Fire Island would destroy one of the last unspoiled shorelines. Noticing Ormsby's increasingly popular platform, state assembly members Prescott Huntington and John Braslow defected from the unified support and voiced opposition to the road.

As this political storm was brewing across Albany and soon in Washington, Fire Island vacationers and homeowners feared that the summer of 1962 would be their last season on an unspoiled island. The fragmented cultures of Fire Island would become a unifying force under Maurice Barbash. Barbash was not only financially invested with his Dunewood development but also emotionally invested through his love of Fire Island's landscape and rustic culture. The successful plan of action Barbash came up with had four components. The first step was to identify all Fire Island stakeholders and individualize what each one would lose if the parkway were constructed. The second step was to create a unified vision for Fire Island that included mainlanders. Moses always successfully argued that access to the waterfront was a battle against elitism. While at a restaurant, Maurice Barbash and Irving Like were struggling to come up with ideas to combat Moses's elitism argument. While talking to Maurice, Irving sketched his ideas on a napkin, and a Fire Island National Seashore kept coming to mind. Both agreed that the best counterargument would be a national seashore because it would transfer waterfront property to public ownership, an idea with which mainlanders could easily agree. The third step was to determine and utilize everyone's personal skills and connections to win the fight against Moses; for decades, the island had attracted the best of the best. The fourth and final step would be to influence a congressman at the federal level to sponsor a bill to create the national seashore. Wainwright had proposed the first national park/ seashore bill, and Barbash believed that Wainwright's Democratic successor, Otis Pike, would be their only shot at sponsorship. Unifying the islanders and accessing their intellectual capital required the creation of a sense of urgency among them. This sense of urgency was created through headlines in various local papers that stated New York lawmakers were unified on the Fire Island Parkway Project and that the landowners of the island should not hold back a decision that benefits Suffolk County as a whole. Once the sense of urgency had set in and a clear design of this plan to save Fire Island had been laid out, Barbash and Like started to divide the leadership roles amongst themselves. Like, a lawyer, remained skeptical of the success of the cause but told Barbash in a sarcastic joke, "some battles are worth the losing fight." Barbash used this phrase as a rebuttal to any islander expressing doubt in the success of the cause.

Across Fire Island, Barbash began to conduct community town hall meetings about Moses's road and the national seashore proposals. Barbash summarized the proposals as the Moses Plan, which built a road through most of the Fire Island towns, and a plan (later referred to as the Udall plan) that would allow the federal government to buy and preserve large tracts of the island for designation as a national seashore. In response to the town hall meetings, Fire Island businesses unified to back the national seashore proposal. All stores, bars and restaurants across the island placed signs in their windows and gave free pins or stickers to patrons to promote the national seashore. Dunewood and surrounding communities assembled volunteers to canvass the Ocean Beach, Ocean Bay Park, Saltaire and Fair Harbor ferries. The volunteers provided prewritten letters of support for a proposed Fire Island National Seashore and a list of state and federal legislators. Following the town hall meetings and after witnessing the success of Barbash and Like's organized activism, local community leaders within the Fire Island villages took notice and started to mobilize.

Davis Park resident Robert Spencer, a New York City artist and activist, was inspired by activist Jane Jacobs and writings that portrayed Robert Moses as an enemy to preservation. Using this inspiration, he organized the communities of Eastern Fire Island against Moses's plan. Many of the city artists were middle- to lower-middle-class. The economic status of these vacationers kept them from owning property, but they still paid rent. The Tenants Emergency Committee to Save Fire Island organized the renters in the artists' communities in the eastern end of the island. Spencer utilized this group of concerned citizens to mobilize renters through party fundraisers that financed the Fire Island Voters Association. At these fundraisers, people would throw pies at cutouts of Moses for a dollar apiece, or people would participate in clambakes. The clams for the fundraiser would be locally harvested to represent the natural resources of the surrounding estuary. Spencer would assign community artists to create signs with short prose pieces about the beauty of selected areas in each community. At the bottom of these signs, bold letters stated: "This area will be paved over for the proposed highway." These signs were displayed during the summer—peak tourist season. Spencer and the Tenants Emergency Committee's activism extended their preservation campaign beyond Long Island to Greenwich Village in New York City.

Informal meetings and fundraisers were held among the famous patrons of the White Horse Tavern. The artist crowd of Greenwich Village and the White Horse Tavern crowd embraced the cause due to their shared memorable vacations on Fire Island.

The communities of Point O' Woods and Saltaire were encouraged to utilize their elite business connections to gain more political influence on the mainland. Saltaire vacationer John Biderman was the skilled marketing director for Bantam Books. His talents became a public relations staple for the Fire Island Voters Association and provided marketing support for a national seashore from elite business circles that bankrolled many state elections. Priscilla Roe, a resident of Point O' Woods and a member of the League of Women Voters, opened a phone campaign to call all state and local officials. When League of Women Voters volunteers felt legislators' aides were screening calls to the targeted officials, Roe got the home phone numbers of the officials and called them in the early morning hours before they left for their offices. The effectiveness of Biderman's lobbying skills and Roe's aggressive phone campaign gradually led state assembly members to sway from Moses's proposed roads and cars plan. Prescott Huntington, Second District assemblyman, who was previously against the Moses Plan, became inspired by the growing grassroots efforts and adopted a more aggressive anti-road stance into his campaign. In an editorial, Huntington wrote that "the highway and the erosion control project are seen as a done deal that are interconnected. In fact the decision is not binding and should not be connected as one. The commission should have an open mind to other proposals."[58]

The Fire Island Community was not limited to renters, staycation visitors and homeowners. Fixtures of the island community included sport and commercial fisherman, nature enthusiasts and dune buggy hobbyists. Claire Siegel, member of the Long Island Beach Buggy Association, was instrumental in organizing and unifying members of the association to support and promote the national seashore proposal. Daily meetings conducted by Siegel started with all the groups and individuals sharing their ideas and hopes for Fire Island. Siegel would point out what the ideas and hopes had in common and promote the concept that a national seashore would be ideal for the shared vision. Groups inspired and called to action by these meetings included the Suffolk and Nassau Fish and Game Association and Conservationists United for Long Island. The collective efforts of these groups resulted in aggressive letter-writing drives to Congressman Otis Pike and a discussion that evolved from dinner-table conversations among sportsmen, sportswomen and family members to mainstream political debates.

The grassroots tactics to preserve Fire Island had to be further exported from family members to special-interest groups. The majority of Long Islanders were unaware of the importance of preserving Fire Island and viewed the island as a destination for an elitist getaway. Like and Barbash attempted to contact all media outlets that would entertain opposition to the parkway—*Newsday, The New York Times, The Islip Bulletin* and all other popular newspapers were under the influence of Moses and advocated support for his projects. The only local paper that had been strongly critical of Robert Moses was the *Babylon Leader.* Thirty years prior to 1962, the paper had fought Moses on obtaining ownership of Oak Island and Captree to build his Ocean Parkway; once again, the *Leader* supported any resistance toward his proposed extension of the parkway. Karl Grossman, a reporter from the *Leader*, became the first to report on the resistance from vacationers and kept daily posts of open town hall meetings for South Shore residents. While Barbash was giving a presentation on the need for the national seashore, Paul Townsend, publisher of the *Long Island Commercial Review*, began to take notice. Getting good press in the *Commercial Review*, an advocate for small-business interests across Long Island, would be a big endorsement; chambers of commerce along the South Shore based their political and economic views almost entirely on the paper. Moses argued that his dune road would bring commerce across the island through rising home values and transportation routes. After follow-up meetings with Townsend, Barbash and Like explained that a national seashore would increase commerce along the South Shore downtowns through more traffic to ferry terminals. This was a big issue due to the growth of malls, which were a growing worry in terms of taking away pedestrian traffic from small downtown stores. With the support of the *Commercial Review* and the chamber of commerce—the backbone of the local Republican Party—the pro-parkway advocates in the county could be swayed. This was a necessity, because the Republican Party controlled the state.

Sensing the shift in views, realizing the benefits of a national seashore to his own community and foreseeing the potential to inflict a Moses loss, Sayville resident and publisher Joseph Jahn of the *Suffolk County News* began a journalistic crusade against the parkway. Daily columns analyzed the negative effects of the parkway on the environment and the taxpayer. In one issue, Jahn reported that Fire Island's Water Island was four hundred feet wide, meaning that all homes across the community would have to be demolished.

The destruction of the community would take many of those homes that use very little public works services off the local tax rolls, which provided a surplus of revenue to the town. This alarmed taxpayers concerned about a substantial loss of local tax revenue and potential deficits for the town.

These allies in the press soon began to make a difference. *Babylon Leader*'s Karl Grossman reported the story that made one of the biggest impacts by not just swaying mainlanders' perspectives on the road through Fire Island but also challenging their trust in Moses. Grossman reported that during the twilight hours, Moses would routinely secretly replace sand that had eroded along the Ocean Parkway after coastal storms. This story debunked Moses's original claim that a parkway could anchor shifting and eroding dunes. The only problem was that Grossman's story gained the attention of only the three papers that supported the cause. To draw more attention to the story, Irving Like filed a lawsuit on the grounds that Moses was hiding the expenditures of the erosion work through the Jones Beach State Parks Authority. Unlike a commission, an authority is a closed entity, so funds spent for this project should have been disclosed through the Long Island Parks Commission. As the lawsuit was being argued in court, Grossman would stake out the parkway after a report of rough seas to investigate how long the work took and what equipment was used. He reported his nightly investigations to Like in an effort to gain more background for Like's suit. Popular newspapers disregarded Grossman, Townsend and Jahn as outliers and followers of Barbash, who were referred to as the anti-roaders, but their efforts were starting to sway influential mainlanders in towns surrounding the Fire Island communities.

The local media attention and grassroots activism across Fire Island and Long Island came to a boiling point during the first public hearing for the proposed road. The mobilizing efforts of the League of Women Voters and the Fire Island Voters Association became very visible, with over one thousand activists showing up on July 10, 1962, at the Jones Beach hearing. The meeting at the West Bathhouse had nine hundred people inside and hundreds more activists outside picketing. The signs of the activists who paraded around Jones Beach and the West Bathhouse read "Ban the Beep" or "Caution: Creeping Concrete." Protesters chanted songs with lyrics such as, "Going to lay my pick and shovel down by the Oceanside and I isn't a-gonna study roads no more."[59] The loudness of the protesters outside was matched by the outrage of the attendees. Charles Lowry, president of the Point O' Woods Association, stated in opening the hearing, "The road is a waste of taxpayers' money. The dunes can be stabilized by conserving all

Bumper sticker that promoted making Fire Island a national seashore. *Karl Grossman Collection.*

the undeveloped land of Fire Island." Moses followed up, outlining his dune road and its benefits for the island, but protesters started shouting, "Moses would save Fire Island the way Hitler saved the Sudetenland."[60] After more than twenty minutes of emotions flaring from the anti-roaders, Moses and state engineers walked out of the meeting, forcing it to adjourn. Media attention surrounding the hearing made state and federal officials take notice. Governor Rockefeller, once a vocal supporter of Moses's projects, began to decline to answer questions as to whether he still supported the Fire Island highway. New York's federal senator Jacob Javits began to question the costs and purpose of constructing the road and refused to endorse the highway project.

Media attention began to sway not only the governor and senator but business leaders as well. Successful businessmen and wealthy local families who had once been friends and supporters of Moses began to publicly voice their support for his opponents. Ward Melville, developer of the Three Village area and a handful of drugstores that became known as the CVS pharmacies, wrote a letter to Moses expressing that the road would be a destructive force to the habitat of Fire Island and suggesting that he support the Udall plan to create a national seashore. The first local business owners who joined the growing support were Doug Brewster, owner of Brewster Boatyard in Bay Shore, and ferryboat owner Kiki Sherman. Brewster and Sherman helped organize nautically-based businesses in an effort to raise money for the Fire Island Voters Association and contact elected officials about the negative economic impact on their businesses that would come from the construction of a highway. When it became more evident that the state was planning to build the highway through the island, Brewster reached out to Bill Marran, owner of Marran Home Oil, who organized other well-to-do business owners to not donate money to politicians who support the Fire

Island Highway in county elections and to pull money from officials who do not support the national seashore.

Moses rallied to seize the offensive, and the media, sensing this could be a losing battle for Moses, began to defect to the anti-road lobby. Editorials in *The New York Times*, *Newsday* and *New York World-Telegram* had consistently supported Moses's previous proposals, but they became opponents of the highway. Dave Balch of the *New York World-Telegram* wrote in his daily editorial that "making more accessible by automobile will share the islands special qualities, but in fact opening the island up to automobiles will destroy its most special quality."[61] In response to the editorial, Moses wrote to Balch, "I spent a large part of my life on Fire Island and know what makes up its special qualities. Fire Island and Jones Beach State Parks accommodates accessibility since 1927." In a *Life* magazine editorial, Moses was called out on his proposal that would displace Fire Island residents. Moses responded to the editorial by denying the claim and calling the article's supporting evidence "a grotesque error." In letters responding to Secretary of the Interior Stewart Udall's call for a national seashore, Moses again requested that he reconsider placing the national seashore on the North Shore instead of South Shore's Fire Island. He reaffirmed the argument that only two sections of the Long Island Sound were in public ownership as opposed to the majority of the South Shore coastline.

In the midst of the media, federal and state turmoil of November 1962, Moses was able to finish construction of his Fire Island inlet bridge. Moses's $5 million expansion of all park facilities and parking lots within Fire Island State Park gave the public a preview of what Fire Island could become. The finished construction of the Fire Island inlet bridge and the Smith's Point Bridge, which was completed in 1959, left the dune road as the only incomplete part of his Ocean Parkway vision. During the celebration for the completion of the inlet bridge, a guest asked Moses if the Fire Island highway would now be constructed; Moses defensively responded by pointing to Fire Island and saying, "Look, the road is meant to be there."[62] Working with Lee Dennison, Moses got Suffolk County to pass legislation for a $750,000 purchase of a ten-mile stretch of Eastern Fire Island. The county designated this section for park use, allowing Moses to build his highway on the entire ten-mile stretch. Pushing for public ownership with no road construction restrictions, Moses began to contact landowners who had sizeable tracts of land within various communities on Fire Island. Moses's efforts to purchase these smaller tracts of land were also designed to undermine community efforts against him. Despite his attempts to bestow monetary gains above market value, property owners farther west stayed stubbornly loyal to the Fire Island communities and did not sell.

Desperate because of his failure to sway landowners and by the evolving support for a national seashore, Moses started a publicized war of words with Secretary of the Interior Stewart Udall. When Udall publicly criticized suburban park designs by stating that preserved land should not have commercialized roads or public facilities, Moses boasted that the unnatural Jones Beach Park replaced a mosquito-infested swamp.[63] Moses's attacks then turned personal against Udall, portraying the secretary as an out-of-towner pushing another state's norm on Long Island. In a *New York Times* interview, Udall responded that "there is nothing like Jones Beach in the entire United States, and we are not interested in pursuing a Jones Beach type of park."[64] Moses viewed this as a backhanded compliment and continued his attacks, which eventually got the full attention of U.S. senator Jacob Javits.

A vacationer on Fire Island, Javits was becoming increasingly alarmed by Moses's plans and publicized attacks. Losing support in the federal government would be a fatal blow to Moses's plan. In New York State, Moses had no limits to his power or oversight, but within the federal government, Moses faced checks from several federal officials who could block federal highway grants. Taking notice of the media attention about the highway and public debates with Udall, Moses tried his old trick of elitism versus the benefits for the average Long Islander. Media outlets that once praised Moses and amplified his anti-elitist rhetoric stayed silent. However, *The Islip Bulletin* remained key to shaping his image within Islip Township. Support within Islip was vital because it was one of two Suffolk County townships with jurisdiction over the proposed Fire Island Highway. *The Bulletin* reported that the counter protestors were "Militant Isolation Champions, or summer residents who were advocating to spend millions of year-round tax dollars to preserve the summer sanctuary of a fortunate few."[65]

Moses's tactic of using anti-elitism to combat Udall and promote his projects was a relic of the past that failed to sway support in the 1960s. The culture of Long Island had changed. Moses's message was for a Long Island locked in battle between its emerging suburban self-image and a nostalgic attempt at holding onto the image of Gilded Age estates. The new Long Island became a collection of communities that had a strong middle class who viewed its scenic waterfront as a birthright and who had become fiercely defensive about preserving it. Local villages and townships changed with the services they provided and the ways they were funded with the development of suburbia. Fire Island served as a great tax base

LEARN TO SWIM CAMPAIGN

JUNE 3 - JUNE 22

CLASSES FOR ALL AGES FORMING IN ALL POOLS
SPONSORED BY DEPARTMENT OF PARKS

Moses's parks would be open to anyone with a car, but he reinforced racial segregation through hiring practices within the parks and the designs of the facilities. Posters on the walls of the park facilities were believed to have symbolic messaging that promoted racial segregation. *Library of Congress.*

for the local towns and counties due to the limited demand for public works, but hurricanes had become increasingly expensive to the state in terms of post-storm cleanups. Many elected officials were eager to keep the tax base but push the cleanup expenses on to someone else. The answer to sharing the financial burden was to allow the development of a national seashore.[66] Though he was once a visionary for the future of Long Island, Moses had become stuck in the past and was oblivious to the needs and demands of the new Long Island.

The beginning of the end for Moses and his road came at the close of 1962. During the early 1960s, Moses and his projects became the center of negative attention. The local media, once his timeless ally, began to sway from Moses's achievements to his race-based hiring practices within his parks and the unchecked power he flaunted. The proposed Lower Manhattan Expressway led to the creation of an organized grassroots effort to protest any new urban reform that conflicted with the character or identity of Manhattan communities. Moses's arrogance toward the Manhattan locals fighting to preserve their community became well known throughout national media, leading to the abandoning of the project. Loss of public esteem and concern about Moses's amassed power became a political liability. Elected officials began making public stands against the unchecked power Moses had wielded over the state for the last thirty years.

Governor Nelson Rockefeller, trying to build his political persona for a possible Republican presidential nomination in 1964, commenced a review of all appointees and policies that could hurt his public image. Moses's hiring practices within his agencies were based on loyalty and nepotism—Rockefeller viewed these practices and the rising negative media attention toward Moses as a potential cancer to his image of good government. The first major challenge to Moses and his power would come in late 1962 from Governor Rockefeller's younger brother, Laurance Rockefeller. Laurance was the founder of the American Conservation Association. His successful activism got the attention of the Kennedy administration, which got him appointed to the Outdoor Recreation Resources Review Commission (ORRRC). While active in the ORRRC, Laurance publicly supported the national seashore proposal and identified Fire Island as one of the top sixteen places in America that should have priority for protection. Laurance's argument to add Fire Island as a top priority was that it was unspoiled nature within miles of a densely populated area. His public stance grew to become a challenge to Moses and his consolidated power within the state. Laurance's view and political action could potentially be a catalyst for opposition to Moses's career goal of a scenic highway. Unbeknownst to Moses, Laurance wanted his position of Long Island Parks commissioner, and his brother, Governor Rockefeller, was waiting for the right opportunity to replace Moses. Outraged over Laurance's public statements on how a four-lane road on Fire Island would conflict with conservation, Moses demanded that Governor Rockefeller silence Laurance's criticism. When Governor Rockefeller refused, Moses threated to resign from three of his state-appointed positions. Not backing down from Moses's challenge, the governor accepted Moses's resignation as chairman of the State Power Authority, chairman of the State Park Council and president of the Long Island State Parks Commission (the Long Island State Parks Commission included the two smaller commissions of Jones Beach State Parkway Authority and Bethpage Park Authority). The following day, Moses went back to Rockefeller's office and told him they both had time to reflect on yesterday's events and that he would take back his resignations. Rockefeller, however, using Moses's outbursts of anger to replace him, refused to let Moses rescind his resignations. Moses, the most powerful person in New York, had met his match. The only positions Moses maintained were president of the New York World's Fair Corporation and Triborough Bridge Authority and representative to Federal-State Highway Construction Projects. Moses would retire from these three remaining positions within ten years. The unchecked power of his career never materialized to monetary gains. At the peak of his career, Moses took a salary of only $10,000 per year from the three positions from which he resigned.

The overall legacy of Moses was his idea of democratizing our scenic landscapes, but it conflicted with the balance of preservation and suburban growth. All of Eastern Nassau and Western Suffolk Counties' canals, boat channels and creeks that flowed into the Great South Bay became polluted from the closing of inlets to construct Ocean Parkway. Prior to the construction of Ocean Parkway, the inlets would flush out the bay and the estuaries with high tide from the ocean. Now, the pollutants of suburbia stayed stagnant in the bay. The pollutants began to kill off the once-bountiful fishing industry on which Long Island had prided itself for centuries. Despite public hearings and concerns from locals, Moses—his power unchecked—ignored the experts. The layout of Moses's roads and parks was centered on his vision of what suburbia and the city should look like and not on what the people that lived there wanted. The visions of locals and Moses became disconnected instead of shared.

In his later years, Moses rented a house on the farthest easternmost section of Oak Beach closest to the Robert Moses Causeway and Park. Moses had the living room of the house redesigned for a view of his Fire Island/Robert Moses Bridge and the Fire Island/Robert Moses Water Tower.[67] When entertaining visitors, Moses would grab a random guest's arm and pull him or her into the living room, standing near the window and saying, "can you see a road is supposed to be there?" in an effort to resurrect one of his biggest defeats.[68] Toward the end of his life, he had become more protective, defending the environmental impact of his projects and rejecting the facts that closing inlets created stagnated pollution in the bays and paved roads are not the best method of preservation.

The preservation of Fire Island become an issue not only about a proposed highway—it was also a referendum on what was environmentally and politically wrong with the suburbia model. Moses was out, but to restore public trust for preservation, Fire Island had to be made right. Governor Rockefeller and elected officials took notice and reacted. During a meeting between Governor Rockefeller and the League of Women Voters, he was asked about the status of the proposed Fire Island Highway. Rockefeller replied, "The decision to build the road will be delayed; we have plenty of parks now, but the erosion control project will go ahead."[69] This delay signaled an opportunity for the federal government to implement a national seashore.

The mainstream political debate shifted to environmentalism and responsible government, with politicians like Manhattan congressman John Lindsay putting the Fire Island National Seashore at the top of their environmental policy stances. Using the national seashore as a platform became a way to flex muscle against Moses's unchecked power and advocate for good government. Many of Lindsay's constituents and donors were vacationers on Fire Island and opponents of the Lower Manhattan

Expressway. Wanting to become New York City's next mayor, Lindsay used the opportunity to introduce the Fire Island National Seashore Bill—as H.R. 4999—to the House of Representatives during the 87th Congress in 1963. Introducing the bill the second time as H.R. 6936 was a longtime supporter of Moses: Otis Pike. Congressman Leo O'Brien of Albany stated in an interview: "This bill has strong support and will take a little more than a half hour to secure approval." In the U.S. Senate, New York senator Javits and cosponsor Senator Kenneth Keating introduced the Fire Island National Seashore Bill to the full Senate for debate. Both proposed bills called for the preservation of 7,500 acres of the island, but neither set a price for the land. The appropriations for the acreage had to be investigated by a subcommittee.

Following the introduction of the Fire Island National Seashore Bill, a senatorial delegation asked to tour the island with the prospects of bipartisan support for the national seashore proposal. This tour included Senator Alan Bible of Nevada, who was the chairman of the subcommittee for the national seashore bill, and other committee members, including Senator Ernest Gruening of Alaska, Senator Leonard B. Jordan of Idaho and Senator Alan Simpson of Wyoming. The focus of the series of visits was to view the natural landscape and look into the cultures of the island communities. Cherry Grove, defined by the media as a place known for "lewd acts," had to rebrand itself during the legislative tours. The preservation of Fire Island was not only a dispute over conservation but also a way to shield the gay and lesbian community from homophobic policies that could threaten the town's existence. Locals viewed the national seashore as a way to provide the needed isolation to keep the residents anonymous from the mainland. This tour had no room for failure. The day before the tour, the head of the Cherry Grove Property Owners' Association had the community conform to present itself as an ideal American resort community. All homes were asked to fly the United States flag in front, and all signs of a gay counterculture were concealed. Thus, Cherry Grove presented itself to the delegation as an artists' community. This new label made lawmakers communicate to their constituents that they were not protecting gays and lesbians but rather an artists' retreat community. At the conclusion of the tour, the committee of senators expressed to the locals that once the bill was passed, "buildings outside developed communities which were built before January 1, 1963, will not be effected."[70] This reassurance that the present communities would remain untouched by the federal government was all the assurance Cherry Grove needed to secure the protected way of life for the locals.

Four-wheel-driving on Fire Island beach. *Queens Borough Public Library, Archives,* Long Island Daily Press *Photograph Morgue Collection.*

Following the congressional visits, legislators were excited about Fire Island's scenes of unspoiled nature, but they had concerns about how to preserve as much land as possible. The finished construction of the Causeway Bridge and state park bathhouses increased annual visitation from 175,000 to 3,000,000 people per year.[71] Access to the national park would be limited to foot and bike trails to avoid the congestion often seen at state parks. Sparsely populated communities east of Davis Park, Skunk Hallow, Whale House Point and Long Cove, as well as private estate resort communities Mud Creek, Bayberry Dunes and Fiddleton, would not be protected or recognized in the national seashore legislation. Residents within these communities would be viewed as squatters, and they would have to vacate the land. Some of the artists who raised money and awareness for preservation efforts inhabited these "squatter communities." Through their efforts, the sunny paradises that they loved would be sacrificed in final legislation. Preservation of additional land was addressed by earmarking $16 million to purchase land along the barrier island and oceanfront. To calm the fears of local inland residents and to appease county and state officials, the final bill asserted that state, county and town parks would

The groundbreaking of the new Fire Island National Seashore, with Stewart Udall holding the ceremonial shovel. Udall signed and presented the photograph to Maurice Barbash. *Susan Barbash Collection.*

remain under present ownership unless they were voluntarily turned over to the federal government.[72]

Environmental lobbying groups such as The Wilderness Society, the National Wildlife Federation, and the Sierra Club wanted input on environmental restrictions for the final draft of the bill. The lobbying efforts of these outside groups would come into conflict with locals' recreational use of the barrier island. Swayed by environmental groups, Congressman Hugh Carey wanted special protection added to the bill for migratory waterfowl. These protections would have limited four-wheel-driving or dune buggy riding on the beach. The Long Island Beach Buggy Association, instrumental in the grassroots efforts to preserve the island as a national seashore, had its access restricted to the beach as an unintended consequence of its preservation efforts.

On September 11, 1964, President Lyndon B. Johnson signed the Fire Island National Seashore Bill, making thirty-three miles of Fire Island a national park. The success of local grassroots organizations in combating a New York State public works project inspired citizen battles over disappearing green space. Groups including the Long Island Environmental Council and the Environmental Defense Fund made inroads into preserving the natural landscape by using the tactics of Barbash and Like, but the empowering feeling of citizens taking ownership over their government outside of non-established groups created a pro-environmental contingency that elected officials had to appease. The reduced environmental impact on Fire Island and its large, wealthiest communities came at the cost of towns east of Davis Park and middle-class recreational groups like the Long Island Beach Buggy Association. Isolating these towns and groups paved the way for a culture of distrusting the federal government and became a thirty-year legal battle to save a way of life from the impacts of the Fire Island National Seashore.

6

ROLLOUT OF FIRE ISLAND NATIONAL SEASHORE

H aving acquired Fire Island, federal conservation specialists became aware of the potential impact of constant environmental changes on the future of their preservation efforts. Some of the issues that federal officials had to address included the fact that 10 percent of the homes were built in dune-protected areas, communities were set up and established based on uncertain land ownership claims, towns must be dissolved for open space preservation and several species that inhabit the island were becoming endangered. One such species that limited access to building along the beaches was the piping plover. Hunted for its feathers, which were used in ladies' hats, the piping plover became known as a threatened species as early as 1918.[73] Hunting of the plover ceased, but the congestion of summer vacationers, trampling of nests, wandering dogs and four-wheel-driving kept the bird's population endangered. Another endangered species that drew attention of policymakers was the seabeach amaranth. The amaranth was becoming extinct due to overdevelopment of summer communities, which limited habitats. Federal officials scrambled to come up with short-term solutions for both of these endangered species, including limiting access to sections of the beach where the plover nests and where amaranth grows, but public ownership conflicts with limiting access. A long-term solution that respects public accessibility was needed but almost impossible to achieve.

For more than six years, Harry Kilthau of Long Cove, Fire Island, had fought against Moses's Fire Island Highway. Throughout that six-year fight against Moses's argument that his highway would be for the public good and should not be sidetracked by the selfish interest of a few privileged people, but after the highway defeat and the creation of a national seashore, Moses's argument was resurrected. The public good became the justification for bulldozing Kilthau's entire community in an effort to create a federal wildlife refuge. Passage of the National Seashore Act allocated funds for the government purchase of 4,500 acres of land. Communities east of Davis Park, including Skunk Hallow, Long Cove and Whalehouse Point, were either built after 1963 outside developed communities or had weak arguments for ownership claims. Further weaknesses in property rights claims of Eastern Fire Island residents were that many of the homes were built on leasehold property. The residents in communities east of Davis Park owned their homes but leased the property. Residents of sixty-five leasehold homes were the first to be targeted for eviction. Federal acquisition officer Leslie W. Piel, who was in charge of acquiring the 4,500 acres for the Fire Island National Seashore, stated that "those who establish rights as squatters by having fifteen years of occupancy had the right to remain there for a maximum of twenty-five years."[74] In an attempt to find a middle ground, the National Park Service and the Eastern Fire Island squatters reached an agreement that residents would vacate their homes by Labor Day 1977. One hundred and fifty squatters claimed rights to the sixty-five homes that were ordered to be vacated, but twenty-four squatters remained behind to fight for their right to stay for their "full term" ending in 1992. The National Park Service fought these leaseholders through settlements, court battles and expanding land claims.

Leading up to Labor Day 1977, dozens of squatters filed appeals against the eviction. Hoping to utilize the distrust between county, state and town officials, squatters fought the federal government's eminent domain clause. Dozens of residents continued their claim of full rights to the land for twenty-five years, hoping to preserve their summer family traditions or at least hold out for better financial compensation for their homes. The courts granted a one-year extension for the squatters to further fight their cases or remove their homes from the land.

The court set the summer of 1978 as the last season for the remaining twenty-one residents of Eastern Fire Island. Some of the squatters decided to capitalize on the last season by subleasing their homes to vacationers, but eight residents—Joseph Felice Sr., Joseph Felice Jr., Louis Felice, Dominick Felice, Patrick Felice, Henry Nagle, Dale Whitlock and Norman Reich—dug in for a lengthy court battle. The legal argument of the remaining squatters became more of a public opinion debate. Fully understanding they were fighting a losing legal battle, the squatters tried swinging public opinion in their favor. Local media highlighted that although their land ownership claims were questionable, they had built the houses and developed the essentials themselves. Dominick Felice stated in an interview with *Newsday* that "this is a fight between the little people and the tentacles of an insensitive federal bureaucracy."[75] Media attention reached Jacob Javits, one of the senators who had pushed the national seashore bill through to legislation. In a press release, Senator Javits stated that he "would look into the conflict and possibly introduce a bill to save the homes." After receiving limited support from his colleagues and having his requests for a delay rejected by Interior Secretary Cecil Andrus, Javits gave up his efforts to save the squatters' houses. The only hope left for the squatters was that public opinion would sway the court's decision.

In September 1978, the squatters lost their appeal. The presiding judge on the case, John R. Bartels, wrote, "It appears that the respondents who spent their vacations for free on another's property for decades have been dealt with more than fairly, and in strict accordance with law by the park service."[76] Within a month, most of the original squatter houses were declared abandoned and scheduled to be demolished. Residents of the cottages protested that they had not abandoned their homes, but their pleas fell on deaf ears. In a last-minute appeal, twenty of the squatter homes were saved until residents' leases and protection rights ran out in 1992. The towns and any municipalities were to be dissolved. The Long Cove homes were the first to be leveled and removed, and by January 25, 1979, only the twenty protected homes remained. The Long Cove, Skunk Hallow and Whalehouse Point communities became memories of a bygone era after sharing their evolutionary beginnings with Ocean Beach, Saltaire, Fair Harbor, Cherry Grove and Kismet.

The 1,363 acres acquired after the destruction of Long Cove, Whalehouse Point and Skunk Hallow became the site of a federally designated wilderness site called the Otis Pike Fire Island High Dune Wilderness. Fire Island's wilderness site became the smallest in size, the closest to a heavily populated area and the only one in New York. For designation under the Wilderness Act, the site had to be "un-trampled by man, and be a place where man himself is a visitor who does not remain."[77] Maintaining the wilderness area requires the least human interference with the natural environment. In 1992, the federal government demolished the remaining twenty cottages and surrendered the sites to the elements of nature. Full preservation of the site expanded from 1,363 to 1,380 acres, encompassing 25 percent of Fire Island.

Before the court battles over the evictions of the squatters and the establishment of the wilderness areas, the National Park Service got into a land ownership dispute between Suffolk County and New York State. In May 1973, the federal government announced it would buy an additional 3,500 acres of Fire Island. These proposed parcels would include Suffolk County's Smith's Point and New York State's Robert Moses State Park (formally known as Fire Island State Park). Suffolk County and its residents—proud of their county-owned access to the oceanfront—became vocal opponents of the proposed extension. Suffolk County's master planner Lee Koppelman stated, "Smith's Point is already in the public domain, and we're not going to give it away to the federal government."[78] Koppelman's argument had a legal base. In accordance with the Fire Island National Seashore agreement, the federal government cannot acquire county or state land unless the county or state agrees to forfeit the land in a sale. The proposed purchase drew mixed feelings from towns that had jurisdiction over Fire Island. The federal government expressed interest in purchasing a seventeen-acre Bellport Village parcel of land and all privately owned beach and dune properties. Federal ownership of all dune and beach property throughout the island, designated a dune district, would not only ban beach buggies on the beach but would also place building regulation of the oceanfront under federal jurisdiction. Islip town supervisor Peter Cohalan issued a public statement that he would reject any purchase of Islip-owned public land but agreed with federal regulation of driving on the beach and development restrictions along the ocean. Similar to the prior argument for the national seashore, the local towns wanted tax revenue from the island summer communities but wanted to provide the least amount of maintenance for the towns. One of the largest costs would be maintaining the dunes and the beaches. Federal ownership would shift these expenses to the federal government and keep local revenue in the town.

The proposed purchases of Fire Island property and the dissolution of eastern island communities had contradictory effects due to the hands-off approach to development within established Fire Island communities. After the creation of the Fire Island National Seashore, the summer resident population increased by 50 percent, creating a demand for new building. Federal limits in development within established communities were all but lifted in the Ocean Beach court case *Dittmer v. Epstein*, which ruled that owners are allowed to build on their property as a necessity. The effects of the case made building variances localized within the village or town municipalities. Bars, grills, rooming houses and movie theaters were built across the island. Proposed multimillion-dollar master plans included a new ferry terminal in mainland Blue Point and a twelve-foot-wide concrete pathway through the center of the island. The master plan gained traction after a federal study highlighted that 70 percent of the island's seasonal visitors came by private boat. These results encouraged elected officials to open a public dialogue about how to make publicly owned land more accessible. Locals opposed the ferry terminal but were most vocal on any road and referred to the concrete pathway as the "miniature Moses Highway."[79] Like the mainland preservation efforts, federal government intervention was controversial, and islanders were hesitant to ask for help in creating stricter regulations after witnessing the struggles of the squatters. Collectively, the concerns of locals were channeled into a lawsuit filed by George Biderman and the Fire Island Voters Association. The lawsuit boldly argued that the U.S. Department of the Interior was not enforcing regulations on building variances. The result of the islanders' concerns blocked the continuation of a constructed concrete path, but the construction of a new ferry terminal in Patchogue within walking distance of the train station increased visitors from 700 per season to 5,100 per season on federally managed land.[80] Accommodating the new seasonal visitors not only brought more economic opportunities but also rapid development. Finding a balance between economic expansion and maintaining small and isolated island charm would be challenging.

Though building variances remained localized within established communities, the newly created dune district made oceanfront homes near dunes vulnerable to federal relocation or demolition. Following the devastating effects of Hurricane Sandy in 2012, rising sea levels became a reality that could no longer be avoided. The future of Fire Island became uncertain as flood maps were redrawn to reflect properties at risk from a projected two- to six-foot rise in sea level. Federal priority in creating a dune line became problematic with every new hurricane and nor'easter, but Sandy was a reality check. Dune replenishment projects necessitated the seizure of dozens of homes through eminent domain.

Hurricane Sandy leveled the entire dune line in the villages of Ocean Bay Park and Davis Park. The federal government condemned more than forty homes and issued seven hundred easements, which permitted building dunes on partial or complete sites of the homes. Robert Spencer, a leading activist who had helped rally and lobby for Fire Island to become a national

Nor'easter damaging a house built in front of the dune line. *Author's collection.*

seashore, had his home of fifty-seven years in Davis Park condemned by the federal government for dune restoration. The $700 million dune replenishment project was to create a dune line at the height of fifteen feet with beach grass and other shrubbery. This would create a root system that would hold the sand together.[81]

The dune line project not only conflicted with homeowners losing their homes but also with other governmental agencies. The piping plover nests on flat, sandy surfaces, and the proposed dune project would limit potential nesting areas. But the concern over the piping plover was dwarfed by Hurricane Sandy's destructiveness in the mainland South Shore communities. Delays of the dune project outraged residents of Mastic Beach, Moriches and Remsenburg. These three low-lying mainland communities suffered significant damage from Sandy. Homeowners in Mastic Beach packed town hall meetings, stating, "the piping plover can find another location to nest while we protect the people."[82] Homeowners' outrage over considering the cancellation of dune replenishment motivated the U.S. Army Corps of Engineers project to be expedited. Altogether, forty-one homes across Fire Island were demolished or relocated for dune restoration.

Storm restoration plans included closing an inlet cut through Fire Island into the bay surrounding Bellport Beach. Prior to Hurricane Sandy's cutting of the inlet, the bay surrounding Bellport Beach was suffering from an influx of brown tides. Like the 1950s resurgence of algae blooms/brown tides, the cause was overflowing septic tanks and limited flow of ocean tides into the bay. Within months of the inlet being cut, the brown tint of the bay became blue, and shellfish populations started to rebound from years of decline. Local fishers started to witness a large influx of striped bass, bluefish, flounder, sea robins and horseshoe crabs. Local environmentalists argued that keeping the inlet open was necessary for maintaining a healthy ecosystem in the bay, and the inlet would close by itself through the natural

House that was slated for demolition to rebuild the dune line. *Author's collection.*

process of longshore drift. However, homeowners in low-lying South Shore communities became concerned over the potential threat of flooding from nor'easters or storm surges.

After making extensive studies, Stony Brook University oceanographic professor Charlie Flagg concluded that the inlet is stable and does not create measurable flooding within South Shore communities. In a rebuttal to

Professor Flagg's conclusions, the Army Corps of Engineers claimed that all breaches of the island create flooding, and to reduce mainland property damage, the new inlet should be filled. As in the debate about local sovereignty versus federal jurisdiction, the research into the inlet's impact came under fire regarding whose study was valid. The final study—accepted by both groups—for keeping the inlet open or closing the inlet was done by the U.S. Geological Survey's St. Petersburg Coastal and Marine Science Center. The only thing USGS concluded as of 2016 was that the inlet will most likely fill in on its own but will take longer than the expected two years due to constant erosion from nor'easters. The debates over the impacts from storm and tidal damage caused by the new inlet and benefits to the ecological balance of the bay are still ongoing.

EPILOGUE

Following the results of the 2016 presidential election, a pro–fossil fuel lobby reversed a decades-old ban on offshore drilling in the Atlantic Ocean. The Trump administration started leasing land for oil and natural gas exploration despite federal impact studies showing that food sources for marine wildlife could be decimated by chemical spills introduced into the ecosystem during the drilling process. Local and state officials are prepared to sue the Trump administration in an effort to block the drilling leases. The federally recognized Shinnecock tribe filed a suit that sovereign standing intergovernmental historic sites could conflict with any fossil fuel exploration.[83] Among the less invasive yet significant proposals with environmental impact is New York State's plan to construct wind farms. In 2017, Governor Andrew Cuomo announced his vision of 2,400 megawatts of offshore windmills that would power over one million homes by 2030. The first step in his proposal was the 2018–2019 goal to have 800 megawatts of offshore windmill energy ready to power a total of 400,000 homes. Later in 2018, communities along the 127 miles of South Shore coastline invited proposals for the construction of wind farms. In return, undisclosed energy companies have submitted proposals for wind farms for up to 40,000 acres located eleven miles offshore. The submitted proposals would generate 400 megawatts—half of the 2018–2019 goal of 800 megawatts. Many environmentalists have been swayed by the benefits of clean and renewable energy for thousands of Long Islanders and artificial reefs that create breeding grounds for various fish species—but often overlooked are concerns about the impact on migratory bird

Surfcasting on Fire Island. *Author's collection.*

populations and disgruntled homeowners whose picturesque views of the ocean could be disrupted by wind farms. Both renewable and nonrenewable energy proposals compete for implementation and are racing to win over public opinion. Town hall meetings with local, state and federal officials have done very little to reduce the community concerns about the new energy proposals. From this public frustration, two forms of activism have emerged. The emerging environmental activists base their activism on cutting-edge scientific research related to rising sea levels and human impact on the ecosystem. Historical preservation activism has been focused on the need to preserve the historically first openly gay community on Fire Island.

During the late 1990s, the Atlantic horseshoe crab began experiencing a steady decline in numbers. Decreasing populations are linked to two main causes. The first is the microalgae bloom caused by high levels of nitrogen from decades of overflowing cesspools. The second is the loss of suitable habitat for the migratory crab population—an irreversible environmental catastrophe. Over the last twenty years, horseshoe crabs have suffered a 1 percent drop in population per year, strongly linked to the 8 percent drop in suitable habitat along Long Island's waterfront.[84] This decline is creating concern among medical researchers, who have conducted thirty years of studies. "*Limulus Amebocyte Lysat*—a chemical found in horseshoe crab blood—triggers a clotting response and seals out invasive bacteria from entering the rest of the crab's system."[85] This chemical spurred a research and economic boom surrounding horseshoe crab blood. Prices of the blood peaked in 2015 at $15,000 per quart. Marine biologists fear that the decline of the horseshoe crab population could not only limit medical research but cause a die-off of migratory East Coast birds, such as red knots and the sanderling, that depend on the 120,000 eggs a female horseshoe crab can lay in one season.

Other species with an uncertain future due to fossil fuel exploration are the green turtle and loggerhead sea turtle. Both species are on the federal threatened or endangered species lists. These turtles usually nest in Florida but graze on algae and sea grass off the coast of Fire Island. Elevated levels of nitrogen from offshore drilling and exploration platforms can stunt the growth of the algae and sea grass upon which these turtles depend. Sea turtles may not have the medical or economic value of horseshoe crabs, but they may be the canary in the coal mine for the lucrative migratory schools of fish that fund the $11 billion sport fishing, commercial fishing and seafood industries that employ 113,000 people in the region.[86]

Declining horseshoe crab populations and threatened grazing grounds for rare sea turtles were not the only concerns for Fire Island preservationists.

Increased coastal storms have battered the island and its protective dunes for decades. Communities face threats from nor'easters and hurricanes that have destroyed homes and historic structures. Following Hurricane Sandy, the state proposed using twenty thousand cubic yards of sand to rebuild dunes and the removal of dozens of homes from the dune line to assure further protection. The condemning of homes created demands for additional protections for culturally significant landmarks still vulnerable to weathering and neglect. Cherry Grove has been the center for the arts and for the gay community for over a century. The Cherry Grove community successfully pioneered the emergence of the LGBT rights movement through an organization unlike other civil rights movements by arguing property rights over gay rights as a first step.[87] The community weathered police raids against gays, hate crimes against gays and the AIDS epidemic. The two cultural testaments in the community that best represent the LGBT movement are the Community House and the Cherry Grove Theater. The Community House held meetings with the Property Owners' Association and American Civil Liberties Union lawyer Benedict Venturo to plan strategies to combat hate crimes and police raids. From these meetings, LGBT rights activism is believed to been exported to the primary residences of vacationers within New York City communities. The Cherry Grove Theater has its place in history due to the LGBT experimental theater. After years of organizing to get landmark status, on June 4, 2013, Cherry Grove's Community House and Cherry Grove Theater were listed in the National Registry of Historic Places. The eligibility requirement cited stated: "Cherry Grove became one of the first and for many years, the only gay and lesbian influenced geography in the United States." The status provides federal priority in preserving the structures for generations to come.

To take the next step in preservation and create further regulation for potential energy exploration of Fire Island, Irving Like, one of the pioneering creators of the national seashore, is working to promote Fire Island as a UNESCO World Heritage site. Like explained: "Similar to the Statue of Liberty, Fire Island is the gateway to New York. Designation does not only protect the site, but allows it to become a global symbol of peace." A UNESCO World Heritage site designation creates a treaty with the United Nations, prioritizing global protection for the recommended site's natural or cultural heritage. According to the United Nations, a World Heritage site has to meet one of the ten criteria set by the World Heritage Convention. There are 1,052 World Heritage sites. These sites include 814 related to culture, 203 based on natural landscapes, and 35 of both cultural

Fire Island Lighthouse covered in snow. *Author's collection.*

and natural significance. Fire Island will fall under the category of both cultural and natural significance, which is referred to as a "mixed use" World Heritage sites. Fire Island could qualify based on at least three of the ten criteria. Irving Like argues that Fire Island fits criteria (vi), (vii) and (ix) for filing a World Heritage site petition.

> *Criterion (vi): To be directly or tangibly associated with events or living traditions, with ideas, or with beliefs, with artistic and literary works of outstanding universal significance.*

The community of Cherry Grove is a symbol of human rights and the origins of the gay rights movement. After World War II, Cherry Grove became one of the first gay and lesbian communities where people could be open about their sexual orientation. Twenty-year Cherry Grove resident Carl Luss stated that "Cherry Grove was the first gay and lesbian resort community which shared rentals and ownership of homes with other gay and lesbian residents and their straight allies." On a national level, the National Register of Historic Places has granted designation to the town's Community House and Cherry Grove Theater. According to the application for the registry, "the Community House and Theater provide an opportunity to document and study the Gay, Lesbian, Bisexual, and Transgender Community in pre-Gay Civil Rights Movement." An example of a cultural tradition practiced throughout the decades is Invasion of the Pines. This forty-year tradition was started by a drag queen named Teri Warren who was refused entry into a restaurant in Pines, Fire Island. As a protest, Warren came back on the Fourth of July with several drag-queen friends to protest the discrimination. This protest became an annual drag queen parade that highlights the pride of Cherry Grove's LGBT community.

Criterion (vii): To contain superlative natural phenomena or areas of exceptional natural beauty and aesthetic importance.

Fire Island Lighthouse is of great aesthetic importance due to its being the first sighting of the United States for transatlantic passengers from Europe during the nineteenth and twentieth centuries.[88] The picturesque views of the Otis Pike Wilderness Area can fit with the exceptional beauty and natural phenomena qualifications. The wilderness area comprises eight miles of sandy beaches bordering high dunes dotted with wildflowers and various species of maritime plants.

Criterion (ix): To be outstanding examples representing significant on-going ecological and biological processes in the evolution and development of terrestrial, fresh water, coastal and marine ecosystems and communities of plants and animals.

The Sunken Forest's three-hundred-year-old maritime holly woodland is ranked globally rare by the National Park Service. American holly, sassafras, shadblow, black cherry, black maple, oak and pitch pine trees comprise the Sunken Forest. This forest matured behind the dunes below sea level. The

Above: Adult buck at Sunken Forest, Fire Island. *Author's collection.*

Right: Harbor seal basking in the sun on the beaches of Sunken Forest. *Author's collection.*

low depressions and trees on this section of the island allowed fresh water to accumulate to create a very distinct ecological system. Accommodated in this space are various threatened or endangered species. The roseate tern and piping plover are endangered in New York State, and the seabeach amaranth plant is on the federal threatened species list.

Attempts to designate Fire Island a World Heritage site are in the very early stages of organizing resources and support. Designation benefits have the Long Island tourism industry at their core. Total tourist revenue generated across Long Island is $5.6 billion supporting 78,000 jobs.[89] The National Park Service's data from 2017 recorded 500,000 visitors to the various towns of Fire Island, and 125,000 additional visitors to the lighthouse spent $19 million. The $19 million figure is not confined just to Fire Island but interconnects with mainland South Shore communities such as Bay Shore, Sayville and Patchogue. These communities have seen their downtowns flourish with the increased tourism to Fire Island's resort communities and beaches. The World Travel and Tourism Council estimated that 12 percent of global GNP is generated through tourism to World Heritage sites.[90] The World Travel and Tourism Council data provide an economic argument that the designation of Fire Island as a World Heritage site will increase tourist revenue on the island and in South Shore mainland towns. The overall intrinsic value of making Fire Island a World Heritage site is what it represents for this generation. Fire Island is symbolic for the LGBT civil rights movement and a battleground for climate change. The economic and environmental benefits are thwarted by the distrust of landowners after the federal government's rollout of the national seashore. Unpopular restrictions on building and recreation can be escalated with federal obligation to maintain designation requirements.

The biggest setback to any designation is not among the sovereignty of property rights but our current political divisions, which prevent bipartisanship. Political officials who pledged their loyalty to their constituents have made way for tribal political affiliations crafted like battle lines in a war. Science and preservation have taken a backseat in the tabloids, and moderate voters have become jaded. Hope could be found in a resurgence of grassroots organizations fueled by young people claiming their spot in history, but so far, many Long Islanders have remained silent or passive. But, as Irving Like stated about the creation of the Fire Island National Seashore, "some battles are worth the losing fight."

NOTES

Introduction

1. Richard Bayles, *Historical and Descriptive Sketches of Suffolk County and Its Towns, Villages, Hamlets, Scenery, Institutions of Important Enterprises with Historical Outline of Long Island From its First Settlements by Europeans* (Port Jefferson, New York: Self-published, 1874); Martha Bockee Flint, *Early Long Island: A Colonial Study* (New York: G.P. Putnam's Sons, 1896), 70; Thomas Bayles, *Early Years Brookhaven Town* (Brookhaven, NY: Bicentennial Commission, 1975), 7.
2. Robert F. Sayre, *Fire Island Past, Present, and Future: The Environmental History of a Barrier Beach* (Iowa City: Oystercatcher Books, 2013), 18.
3. Peter Ross, *History of Long Island, from Its Earliest Settlement to Present Time*, Vol. 1 (New York: Lewis Publishing Company, 1903), 21.
4. Madeleine C. Johnson, *Fire Island: 1650s–1980s* (Mountainside, NJ: Shoreland Press, 1983), 16.
5. Lee E. Koppelman and Seth Forman, *The Fire Island National Seashore: A History* (Albany: State University of New York Press, 2008), 2.
6. U.S. Office of Ocean and Coastal Resource Management, *Village of Ocean Beach Local Waterfront Revitalization Program* (Ocean Beach, NY: Ocean Beach trustees, 2011), 3.
7. U.S. Department of the Interior, National Park Service, *National Register of Historic Places, Cherry Grove Community House and Theater*, by Carl Luss (New York: Cherry Grove Community Association Inc., 2013), Section 8-3.
8. Ibid., Section 8-5.
9. Esther Newton, *Cherry Grove, Fire Island: Sixty Years in America's First Gay and Lesbian Town*, (Durham, NC: Duke University Press, 2014), 48.
10. Johnson, *Fire Island*, 120.

Chapter 1: Robert Moses and His Rise to Power

11. Robert Caro, *The Power Broker: Robert Moses and the Fall of New York* (New York: Vintage Books, 1974), 31.

12. Anthony Flint, *Wrestling with Moses: How Jane Jacobs Took on New York's Master Builder and Transformed the American City* (New York: Random House, 2009), 37.

13. Flint, *Wrestling with Moses*, 41.

14. Vivienne Walt, "Mary Grady Moses, at 77, Widow of Builder Robert Moses," *Newsday* (Melville, NY), September 3, 1993, A62.

Chapter 2: Moses's Vision for the Barrier Islands

15. Caro, *The Power Broker*, 161.

16. Ibid.

17. Tom Morris, *Island of Content: A History of Oak Island, Oak Island Beach and Captree Island, New York* (Babylon, NY: Town of Babylon Office of Historical Services, 2016), 47.

18. Robert Moses, "Opposition to the Captree Causeway," *Long Island Press*, November 1, 1930.

19. Louis Sherwin, "Boulevard Will Mar Life on Strand," *Babylon Leader*, July 25, 1930.

20. Johnson, *Fire Island*, 166.

21. Ibid., 167.

22. "The Town Should Reclaim Its Insular Possessions," *Babylon Leader*, September 29, 1938.

23. "Supervisors Vote Down Moses' Plan, Adopt Own $100,000 Beach Repair Idea," *The Mid-Island Mail* (Medford Station, NY), November 2, 1938.

24. Harold Willmott, letter to the editor, *Brooklyn Daily Eagle*, November 4, 1938.

Chapter 3: Moses's Fight against a Fire Island National Park

25. "Twentieth Century Statistics," 1998, accessed September 9, 2017, https://www.census.gov/prod/99pubs/99statab/sec31.pdf.

26. Langdon Smith, "Democratizing Nature Through State Park Development," *Historical Geography Journal*, vol. 41, 2013.

27. Walt Brevig, "Town Hits Moses' South Shore Inlet Plan," *Newsday*, December 31, 1955, 8.

28. Art Bergmann, "Washington Bureau, Dredge Fire Island Inlet as Aid to CD, State, Wainwright Urges," *Newsday*, May 26, 1953, 7.

29. Tom Morris, "Moses' Inlet Plan Pours Money in Rat Hole: Study," *Newsday*, November 15, 1955, 5.

30. Robert Moses to Governor Averell Harriman, March 6, 1957, New York Public Library Archives, New York City, Robert Moses Papers, Box 8.

31. Robert Moses to Federal Senator Jacob Javits, June 18, 1959, New York Public Library Archives, New York City, Robert Moses Papers, Box 8.
32. Christopher Sellers, *Crabgrass Crucible* (Chapel Hill: University of North Carolina Press, 2012), 99.

Chapter 4 : Development with Limitations

33. Ibid., 46.
34. Adam Rome, *The Bulldozer in the Countryside* (New York: Cambridge University Press, 2001), 121.
35. Ibid., 8.
36. U.S. Fish and Wildlife Service, Department of the Interior, *Status and Trends of Wetlands in the Long Island Sound Area*, by Georgia Basso, 2011, 6–37.
37. James Barron, "At Bottom, Long Island Sound Is a Mess," *The New York Times*, September 11, 1983, A20.
38. Harry Pearson, "Beach Pollution Increased in 73," *Newsday*, June 22, 1974, 3.
39. Ibid.
40. Charles Gorr, "Polluted Water? Then Blame the Detergents," *Newsday*, January 27, 1962, 18.
41. Harry Pearson, "Long Island Runs Up a Bill With Nature," *Newsday*, April 20, 1970, 5.
42. Rome, *Bulldozer in the Countryside*, 123.
43. Special to *Newsday*, "Rocky Asks Bond to Fight Pollution," *Newsday*, December 28, 1964, 11.

Chapter 5: The Defeat of Moses and the Making of a National Seashore

44. Sellers, *Crabgrass Crucible*, 96.
45. Tom Morris in discussion with the author, Babylon Village, August 15, 2017.
46. Bob Spencer in discussion with the author, Bay Shore, July 19, 2017.
47. Robert Moses to Robert MacCrate, counsel to the governor, November 25, 1960, New York Public Library Archives, New York City, Robert Moses Papers, Box 8.
48. Waldo Hutchins to Robert Moses, July 25, 1961, New York Public Library Archives, New York City, Robert Moses Papers, Box 111.
49. Robert Moses to Waldo Hutchins, July 26, 1961, New York Public Library Archives, New York City, Robert Moses Papers, Box 111.
50. Sidney Shapiro to Robert Moses, November 21, 1960, New York Public Library Archives, New York City, Robert Moses Papers, Box 111.
51. Robert Moses, "Moses Road Will Be Similar to a Dike," *The New York Times*, March 6, 1962.

52. State of New York, Commission on the Protection and Preservation of the Atlantic Shore Front, New York State Public Works, *"Protection and Preservation of the Atlantic Shore Front,"* by Robert Moses, compiled by Joseph Carlino, July 27, 1962.

53. Legislature of the State of New York, Temporary State Commission on Protection and Preservation of the Atlantic Shore Front, *"The Protection and Preservation of the Atlantic Shore Front of the State of New York Final Report,"* edited by Joseph Carlino, Rept. NY: Legislature of the State of New York, July 27, 1962.

54. Koppelman and Forman, *Fire Island National Seashore*, 58.

55. Ibid., 68.

56. "Beach Residents Form Voting Unit," *Suffolk County News*, March 23, 1961, 6.

57. Robert Moses telegram to Stewart Udall, June 21, 1962, New York Public Library Archives, New York City, Robert Moses Papers, Box 111.

58. Prescott Huntington, "Fire Island Road: The Verdict's Not Yet In," *Newsday*, August 3, 1962.

59. Robert Wiemer, "Young Fire Islanders Sing Out Opposition," *Newsday*, July 10, 1962.

60. Byron Porterfield, "Moses Quits Fire Island Hearing," *Newsday*, July 10, 1962.

61. Dave Balch, "Let Nature Prevail," *New York World-Telegram*, June, 28, 1962.

62. Tom Morris in discussion with the author, Babylon Village, August 15, 2017.

63. Robert Moses, "Memorandum by Robert Moses on the Future of Fire Island," October 24, 1963, 5 Javits Collection, SBUL, Series 2, Box 78.

64. Ronald Maiorana, "Udall Doubts U.S. Will Buy on L.I.: Suggests It Is Too Late for Purchasing Shore Area," *The New York Times*, June 3, 1962, 56.

65. Jacqueline Mullen, "Coastal Parks for a Metropolitan Nation: How Postwar Politics and Urban Growth Shaped America's Shores" (dissertation submitted to University of Albany, State University of New York), 2015, 222.

66. Ibid., 225.

67. "Robert Caro on the Fall of New York, and Glenn Close on Complicated Characters," *New Yorker* Radio Hour, WNYC, May 4, 2018.

68. Ibid.

69. Stan Hinden, "No Fire Island Road in 63: GOV," *Newsday*, February 26, 1963.

70. Alan Eysen, "Optimistic Senators Tour Fire Island," *Newsday*, June 29, 1963.

71. Ned Kaufman, "Land Regulation at Fire Island National Seashore, A History and Analysis, 1964–2004," U.S. Department of the Interior, September 2008.

72. Newsday Washington Bureau, "Fire Island Shore Bill Is Signed by Johnson," *Newsday*, September 12, 1964.

Chapter 6: Rollout of Fire Island National Seashore

73. Shoshanna McCollum, "Not Just a Dead Bird," *Suffolk County News*, May 19, 2005, 7.
74. "He Gains Park, Loses a Home on Fire Island," *Newsday*, April 16, 1968, 15.
75. Susan Page, "The Little People Vs. the Public Good," *Newsday*, July 13, 1978, 1A.
76. Susan Page, "Fire Island Squatters Lose," *Newsday*, September 15, 1978, 21Q.
77. *A Prospectus for Wilderness in the 8-Mile Zone of the Fire Island National Seashore*, report, Bellport, NY: Fire Island Wilderness Committee, 1980, 2–3.
78. Roberts Fresco, "U.S. Seeks Fire Island Lands: 3,500 Acres Would Be Added to National Park," *Newsday*, May 14, 1973, 3.
79. "From Creation to Crisis," *Suffolk County News*, August 10, 1978, 13.
80. Koppelman and Forman, *Fire Island National Seashore*, 138.
81. Joseph Berger, "Complaints and Warnings about Plan to Replenish Fire Island's Dunes," *New York Times*, May 27, 2014, A3.
82. Ibid.

Epilogue

83. Mark Harrington, "Long Islanders Voice Opposition to Trump's Offshore Drilling Plan," *Newsday*, February 14, 2018.
84. Michael Dobie, "Horseshoe Crabs' Hard-Shell Truth," *Newsday*, July 2, 2017.
85. Samantha Olson, "As Horseshoe Crab Populations Steadily Decrease, the Indispensable Medical Use Is Threatened," *Medical Daily*, May 7, 2014, http://www.medicaldaily.com/horseshoe-crab-populations-steadily-decrease-their-indespensable-medical-use-threatened-280728.
86. U.S. Fish and Wildlife Service, 1997; NMFS, 2000c; Great Lakes Fishery Commission, 2000; USDA, 2000; Appendix C; and estimates by TechLaw.
87. Carl Luss in discussion with the author, Bay Shore, September 15, 2017.
88. Thomas McGann, "Fire Island National Seashore as a World Heritage Site?," *Fire Island News*, April 28, 2016, 12.
89. Ken Schachter, "Tourism Officials Want to Bring the World to Long Island," *Newsday*, September 15, 2017, A5.
90. McGann, "Fire Island National Seashore."

BIBLIOGRAPHY

Andrews, Earle. "Report on Plan to Restore and Protect Fire Island." W. Earle Andrews Engineer Corp., New York, October 1938.

Babylon Leader. "The Town Should Reclaim Its Insular Possessions." September 29, 1938.

Barbash, Maurice. Citizens' Committee for a Fire Island National Seashore. 1962. Citizen petition for National Seashore, Babylon, New York.

Balch, Dave. "Let Nature Prevail." *New York World Telegram,* June, 28, 1962.

Barron, James. "At Bottom, Long Island Sound Is a Mess." *The New York Times,* September 11, 1983.

Bayles, Richard. *Historical and Descriptive Sketches of Suffolk County and Its Towns, Villages, Hamlets, Scenery, Institutions of Important Enterprises with Historical Outline of Long Island From Its First Settlements by Europeans.* Port Jefferson, NY: Self-published, 1874.

———. "Island Geographical Curiosities." Long Island forum, November 1964.

Bayles, Thomas. "Early Years Brookhaven Town." Brookhaven, NY: Bicentennial Commission, 1975.

Berger, Joseph. "Complaints and Warnings about Plan to Replenish Fire Island's Dunes." *The New York Times,* May 27, 2014. 21

Bergmann, Art. "Washington Bureau, Dredge Fire Island Inlet as Aid to CD, State, Wainwright Urges." *Newsday,* May 26, 1953.

Bovino, Arthur. "George Biderman, 81, Organizer against Highway on Fire Island." *The New York Times,* July 26, 2002.

Brawley, Arthur. "The Fire on New York's Famous Little Island." *Sports Illustrated,* July 23, 1962, 42–44.

Brevig, Walt. "Town Hits Moses' South Shore Inlet Plan." *Newsday,* December 31, 1955.

Caro, Robert. *The Power Broker: Robert Moses and the Fall of New York.* New York: Vintage Books, 1974.

————. "Robert Caro on the Fall of New York, and Glenn Close on Complicated Characters." *New Yorker* Radio Hour. WNYC. May 4, 2018.

Chalifoux, Rick. "Revisiting a Critical Time in Fire Island History." *Suffolk County News*, August 6, 2015.

Dobie, Michael. "Horseshoe Crabs' Hard-Shell Truth." *Newsday*, July, 2 2017.

Eysen, Alan. "Optimistic Senators Tour Fire Island." *Newsday*, June 29, 1963.

"Fire Island National Seashore Short-term Community Storm Protection Plan and Environmental Assessment." U.S. Department of the Interior, National Park Service, June 2003.

Flint, Anthony. *Wrestling with Moses: How Jane Jacobs Took on New York's Master Builder and Transformed the American City*. New York: Random House, 2009.

Flint, Martha Bockee. *Early Long Island: A Colonial Study*. New York: G.P. Putnam's Sons, 1896.

Gorr, Charles. "Polluted Water? Then Blame the Detergents." *Newsday*, January 27, 1962.

Grossman, Karl. "Suffolk Close up: Taking on Mr. Moses." *Shelter Island Reporter*, June 29, 2011.

Harrington, Mark. "Long Islanders Voice Opposition to Trump's Offshore Drilling Plan." *Newsday*, February 14, 2018.

Hinden, Stan. "No Fire Island Road in 63: GOV." *Newsday*, February 26, 1963.

Howard, Arthur. "Hurricane Modification of the Offshore Bar of Long Island, New York," *Geographical Review* 29, no. 3, (1939): 400–415.

Huntington, Prescott. "Fire Island Road: The Verdict's Not Yet In." *Newsday*, August 3, 1962.

Hutchins, Waldo. Letter to Robert Moses. July 25, 1961. New York Public Library Archives, New York City. Robert Moses Papers, Box 111.

Johnson, Madeleine C. *Fire Island: 1650s–1980s*. Mountainside, NJ: Shoreland Press, 1983.

Kaufman, Ned. "Land Regulation at Fire Island National Seashore, A History and Analysis, 1964–2004." U.S. Department of the Interior, September 2008.

Kleinfield, N.R. "Otis Pike, 92, Dies: Long Island Congressman Took On CIA." *The New York Times*, January 20, 2014.

Koppelman, Lee E., and Seth Forman. *The Fire Island National Seashore: A History*. Albany: State University of New York Press, 2008.

Legislature of the State of New York. Temporary State Commission on Protection and Preservation of the Atlantic Shore Front. The Protection and Preservation of the Atlantic Shore Front of the State of New York—Final Report. Edited by Joseph Carlino. Rept. NY: Legislature of the State of New York, July 27, 1962.

Letter and attached memorandum from Coulter Young to Robert Moses. July 10, 1930. New York Public Library Box 107, New York City.

Letter and attached memorandum from Robert Moses as Chairman of Triborough Bridge and Tunnel Authority to Senator Javits, October 24, 1963. New York Public Library Box 108, New York City.

Letter and attached memorandum from Robert Moses as Long Island State Park Commission Chairman to Arnold Douglas. August 8, 1955. New York Public Library Box 108, New York City.

Letter and attached memorandum from Robert Moses as Long Island State Park Commission Chairman to Conrad Wirth Director of National Park Service. August 16, 1955. New York Public Library Box 108, New York City.

Letter and attached memorandum from Robert Moses as Long Island State Park Commission Chairman to Town of Islip Board. April 19, 1955. New York Public Library Box 108, New York City.

Letter and attached memorandum from Robert Moses to Coulter Young. July 9, 1930. New York Public Library Box 107, New York City.

Maiorana, Ronald. "Udall Doubts U.S. Will Buy on L.I.: Suggests It Is Too Late for Purchasing Shore Area." *The New York Times*, June 3, 1962.

McCollum, Shoshanna. "Not Just a Dead Bird." *Suffolk County News*, May 19, 2005.

McGann, Thomas. "Fire Island National Seashore as a World Heritage Site?" *Fire Island News*, April 28, 2016.

———. "History: Life on Fire Island." *Fire Island News*, August 29, 2017.

Memorandum: Moriches and Shinnecock Inlet: Robert Moses as Long Island State Park Commission Chairman to Sidney Shapiro. December 10, 1957. New York Public Library Box 108, New York City.

Molotsky, Irvin. "The Fence at Point O'Woods." *The New York Times*, August 28, 1977.

Morris, Tom. Discussion with the author. Babylon Village, August 15, 2017.

———. *Island of Content: A History of Oak Island, Oak Island Beach and Captree Island, New York*. Town of Babylon, Office of Historical Services, Babylon, New York, 2016.

———. "Moses' Inlet Plan Pours Money in Rat Hole: Study." *Newsday*, November 15, 1955.

Moses, Robert. Letter to New York Governor Averell Harriman. March 6, 1957. New York Public Library Archives, New York City. Robert Moses Papers, Box 8.

———. Letter to Robert MacCrate, Counsel to the Governor. November 25, 1960. New York Public Library Archives, New York City. Robert Moses Papers, Box 8.

———. Letter to Stewart Udall. June 21, 1962, Telegram. New York Public Library Archives, New York City. Robert Moses Papers, Box 111.

———. Letter to U.S. Senator Jacob Javits. June 18, 1959. New York Public Library Archives, New York City. Robert Moses Papers, Box 8.

———. Letter to Waldo Hutchins. July 26, 1961. New York Public Library Archives, New York City. Robert Moses Papers, Box 111.

———. "Memorandum by Robert Moses on the Future of Fire Island." October 24, 1963, 5 Javits Collection, SBUL, Series 2, Box 78.

———. "Moses' Road Will Be Similar to a Dike." *The New York Times*, March 6, 1962.

———. "Opposition to the Captree Causeway." *Long Island Press*, November 1, 1930.

Mullen, Jacqueline. "Ash Wednesday on Fire Island." *New York Archives* 13, no. 2, 23–27.

———. "Coastal Parks for a Metropolitan Nation: How Postwar Politics and Urban Growth Shaped America's Shores." Ph.D. dissertation, University of Albany, New York, 2015, Accessed through ProQuest.

National Oceanic and Atmospheric Administration. "Village of Ocean Beach Local Waterfront Revitalization Program." U.S. Office of Ocean and Costal Resource Management, April 8, 2011

Newsday. "He Gains Park, Loses a Home on Fire Island." April 16, 1968.

———. "Special to Newsday, Rocky Asks Bond to Fight Pollution." December 28, 1964.

Newsday Washington Bureau. "Fire Island Shore Bill Is Signed by Johnson." *Newsday*, September 12, 1964.

Newton, Esther. *Cherry Grove, Fire Island: Sixty Years in America's First Gay and Lesbian Town*. Durham, NC: Duke University Press, 2014.

Olson, Samantha. "As Horseshoe Crab Populations Steadily Decrease, the Indispensable Medical Use Is Threatened." *Medical Daily*, May 7, 2014. http://www.medicaldaily.com/horseshoe-crab-populations-steadily-decrease-their-indespensable-medical-use-threatened-280728.

Osborne, Chester. "Changing Shore Lines." *Long Island Forum*, July 1958, 125–126.

Page, Susan. "Fire Island Squatters Lose." *Newsday*, September 15, 1978.

———. "The Little People vs. the Public Good." *Newsday*, July 13, 1978.

Panner, Vicky. "Javits, Pike Open Hearing on Fire Island Shore Bill." *Long Island Commercial Review*, October 1, 1963.

Pearson, Harry. "Beach Pollution Increased in 73." *Newsday*, June 22, 1974.

———. "Long Island Runs Up a Bill with Nature." *Newsday*, April 20, 1970.

Porterfield, Byron. "Moses Quits Fire Island Hearing." *Newsday*, July 10, 1962.

———. "U.S. Seeks to Bar Park Site Homes." *The New York Times*, October 20, 1964.

Powell, Michael. "A Tale of Two Cities." *The New York Times*, May 6, 2007.

"A Prospectus for Wilderness in the 8-Mile Zone of the Fire Island National Seashore." Report. Bellport, NY: Fire Island Wilderness Committee, 1980.

Roberts, Fresco. "U.S. Seeks Fire Island Lands: 3500 Acres Would Be Added to National Park." *Newsday*, May 14, 1973.

Rogers, Cleveland. "Fire Island Hails Abandonment of Ocean Highway." *Brooklyn Daily Eagle*, July 10, 1930, 10.

———. "Urge Parkway Link to Span." *Brooklyn Daily Eagle*, June 16, 1930, 4.

Rome, Adam. *The Bulldozer in the Countryside*. New York: Cambridge University Press, 2001.

Ross, Peter. *History of Long Island, from Its Earliest Settlement to Present Time, vol. 1*. New York: Lewis Publishing Company, 1903.

Sayre, Robert. *Fire Island Past, Present, and Future, The Environmental History of a Barrier Island*. Iowa City, Iowa: Oystercatcher Books, 2013.

Schachter, Ken. "Tourism Officials Want to Bring the World to Long Island." *Newsday*, September 15, 2017.

Sellers, Christopher. *Crabgrass Crucible*. Chapel Hill: The University of North Carolina Press, 2012.

Shapiro, Sidney. Letter to Robert Moses. November 21, 1960. New York Public Library Archives, New York City. Robert Moses Papers, Box 111.

Sherwin, Louis. "Boulevard Will Mar Life on Strand." *Babylon Leader*, July 25, 1930.

Smith, Langdon. "Democratizing Nature Through State Park Development." *Historical Geography Journal*, vol. 41 (2013), 623–640

Spencer, Bob. Discussion with the author. Bay Shore, July 19, 2017.

State of New York. Commission on the Protection and Preservation of the Atlantic Shore Front. New York State Public Works. Protection and Preservation of the Atlantic Shore Front. By Robert Moses. Compiled by Joseph Carlino

Suffolk County News. "Beach Residents Form Voting Unit." March 23, 1961.

———. "From Creation to Crisis." August 10, 1978.

"Supervisors Vote Down Moses' Plan, Adopt Own $100,000 Beach Repair Idea." *The Mid-Island Mail*, November 2, 1938.

Sutter, Paul. *Driven Wild: How the Fight against Automobiles Launched the Modern Wilderness Movement*. Seattle: Seattle University of Washington Press, 2002.

Suydam, Charles. "Fire Island's Changing Lines." *Long Island Forum*, April 1942, 73–74.

Tanski, Jay. "Long Island's Dynamic South Shore, a Primer on the Forces and Trends Shaping Our Coast." Sea Grant New York Extension Program, 2007.

Turnage, William. Comments on the Preliminary Wilderness Proposal for the Fire Island National Seashore, The Wilderness Society, 1983.

"Twentieth Century Statistics." 1998. Accessed September 9, 2017. https://www.census.gov/prod/99pubs/99statab/sec31.pdf.

U.S. Army Corps of Engineers. "Fire Island Inlet to Montauk Point Reformulation Study, U.S. Army Corps of Engineers, New York District, July 2016."

———. "Fire Island Inlet to Moriches Inlet: Fire Island Stabilization Project, Evaluation of Storm Risk Management." Army Corps of Engineers, New York District, June 2014.

U.S. Department of the Interior. National Park Service. National Register of Historic Places, Cherry Grove Community House and Theater, by Carl Luss. New York: Cherry Grove Community Association, Inc., 2013.

U.S. Fish and Wildlife Service, 1997; NMFS, 2000c; Great Lakes Fishery Commission, 2000; USDA, 2000; Appendix C; and estimates by TechLaw.

U.S. Fish and Wildlife Service. Department of the Interior. "Status and Trends of Wetlands in the Long Island Sound Area," by Georgia Basso. 2011.

U.S. House Committee on Interior and Insular Affairs. H.R. 4999, March 18, 1963.

U.S. Office of Ocean and Coastal Resource Management. Village of Ocean Beach Local Waterfront Revitalization Program. Ocean Beach, NY: Ocean Beach Trustees, 2011.

U.S. Senate Committee on Interior and Insular Affairs. S. 1365, April 25, 1963.

Vitello, Paul. "Maurice Barbash, Who Saved Fire Island's Terrain, Dies at 88." *The New York Times*, March 21, 2013.

Walt, Vivienne, "Mary Grady Moses, At 77, Widow of Builder Robert Moses." *Newsday*, September 3, 1993, A62.

Weaver, Warren. "Fire Island Bill near Completion." *The New York Times*, April 11, 1964.

Wiemer, Robert. "Young Fire Islanders Sing Out Opposition." *Newsday*, July 10, 1962.

Willmott, Harold. Letter to the editor. *Brooklyn Daily Eagle*, November 4, 1938.

"World Heritage Status Opportunity for Economic Gain." World Heritage Status. 2009. Accessed July 9, 2017. http://icomos.fa.utl.pt/documentos/2009/WHSTheEconomicGainFinalReport.pdf

ABOUT THE AUTHOR

C hristopher Verga is an instructor of Long Island History, Foundations of American History at Suffolk Community College and a contributor to the online local news sites Greater Babylon, Greater Bay Shore and Greater Patchogue. His published works include the Arcadia Publishing titles Images of America: *Civil Rights on Long Island* and Images of America: *Bay Shore*. Christopher has his educational doctorate from St. John's University. His dissertation work focused on Long Island Native Americans and the impact of tribal recognition within their cultural identity.

Visit us at
www.historypress.com